Reorganizing U.S. Domestic Intelligence

Assessing the Options

GREGORY F. TREVERTON

Prepared for the Department of Homeland Security

RAND HOMELAND SECURITY PROGRAM and
the INTELLIGENCE POLICY CENTER

This research was sponsored by the United States Department of Homeland Security and was conducted jointly under the auspices of the Homeland Security Program within RAND Infrastructure, Safety, and Environment and the Intelligence Policy Center of the RAND National Security Research Division.

Library of Congress Cataloging-in-Publication Data

Treverton, Gregory F.
Reorganizing U.S. domestic intelligence : assessing the options/ Gregory F. Treverton.
p. cm.
Includes bibliographical references.
ISBN 978-0-8330-4501-0 (pbk. : alk. paper)
1. Intelligence service—United States. 2. Terrorism—United States—Prevention. 3. Terrorism—Government policy—United States. I. Title.

JK468.I6T712 2008
363.325'1630973—dc22

2008026150

Cover design by Pete Soriano

Published 2008 by the RAND Corporation
1776 Main Street, P.O. Box 2138, Santa Monica, CA 90407-2138
1200 South Hayes Street, Arlington, VA 22202-5050
4570 Fifth Avenue, Suite 600, Pittsburgh, PA 15213-2665
RAND URL: http://www.rand.org/
To order RAND documents or to obtain additional information, contact
Distribution Services: Telephone: (310) 451-7002;
Fax: (310) 451-6915; Email: order@rand.org

Preface

Terrorism remains prominent on the national agenda, and whether the country's prevention efforts match the threat we face stands central in policy debate. One element of this debate is questioning whether the United States, like some other countries, needs a dedicated domestic intelligence agency. Congress directed that the Department of Homeland Security (DHS) Office of Intelligence and Analysis perform "an independent study on the feasibility of creating a counter terrorism intelligence agency" to examine this issue (U.S. House of Representatives, 2006, p. 122). This report provides a framework for debate and culminates in a discussion of the pros and cons of creating such an agency.

RAND was explicitly asked to frame the issues but not make a recommendation. While we were asked to evaluate U.S. domestic arrangements in general, specific evaluations of particular agencies and their performance were not part of our charter. In particular, while we discuss the FBI's transformation initiatives, an evaluation of that transformation was beyond our charter. Such an independent evaluation would be valuable. The fact that the transformation is very much a work in progress did, however, complicate our task in framing the issues, for much of the public debate is still rooted in pre–September 11 conceptions of the shortcomings of the domestic intelligence enterprise in the United States.

This document aims to enrich the discussion among homeland security policymakers, state and local governments, law enforcement organizations, civil rights and civil liberties organizations, and private sector organizations with interests in homeland security. This study is part of a larger body of RAND research related to homeland security, intelligence, and terrorism. Related RAND publications include the following:

- Peter Chalk and William Rosenau, *Confronting "the Enemy Within": Security Intelligence, the Police, and Counterterrorism in Four Democracies*, MG-100-RC, 2004.
- K. Jack Riley, Gregory F. Treverton, Jeremy M. Wilson, Lois M. Davis, *State and Local Intelligence in the War on Terrorism*, MG-394-RC, 2005.
- Brian A. Jackson, Peter Chalk, Kim Cragin, Bruce Newsome, John V. Parachini, William Rosenau, Erin M. Simpson, Melanie Sisson, and Donald Temple, *Breaching the Fortress Wall: Understanding Terrorist Efforts to Overcome Defensive Technologies*, MG-481-DHS, 2007.

The RAND Homeland Security Program

This research was conducted jointly under the auspices of the Homeland Security Program within RAND Infrastructure, Safety, and Environment and the Intelligence Policy Center of the National Security Research Division. The mission of RAND Infrastructure, Safety, and Environment is to improve the development, operation, use, and protection of society's essential physical assets and natural resources and to enhance the related social assets of safety and security of individuals in transit and in their workplaces and communities. Homeland Security Program research supports the Department of Homeland Security and other agencies charged with preventing and mitigating the effects of terrorist activity within U.S. borders. Projects address critical infrastructure protection, emergency management, terrorism risk management, border control, first responders and preparedness, domestic threat assessments, domestic intelligence, and workforce and training.

Information about the Homeland Security Program is available online (http://www.rand.org/ise/security/). Inquiries about homeland security research projects should be addressed to:

Andrew Morral, Director
Homeland Security Program, ISE
RAND Corporation
1200 South Hayes Street
Arlington, VA 22202-5050
703-413-1100, x5119
Andrew_Morral@rand.org

The RAND Intelligence Policy Center

The Intelligence Policy Center is part of the RAND National Security Research Division (NSRD). NSRD conducts research and analysis for the Office of the Secretary of Defense, the Joint Staff, the Unified Combatant Commands, the defense agencies, the Department of the Navy, the Marine Corps, the U.S. Coast Guard, the U.S. Intelligence Community, allied foreign governments, and foundations.

For more information on RAND's Intelligence Policy Center, address queries to:

John Parachini, Director
Intelligence Policy Center
RAND Corporation
1200 South Hayes Street
Arlington, VA 22202-5050
703-413-1100, x5579
johnvp@rand.org

More information about RAND is available at www.rand.org.

Contents

Figures and Tables

Figures

Tables

Summary

September 11 drove home all too graphically the vulnerability of the United States to terrorism. One among several critical vulnerabilities was poor tactical intelligence. The signals of the September 11 attack went unassembled, and the tocsin of specific warning did not sound. In the wake of that failure, one of the questions on the U.S. agenda in the fight against terrorism is whether the country needs a dedicated domestic intelligence agency separate from law enforcement, on the model of many comparable democracies.

To examine this issue, Congress directed that the Department of Homeland Security Office of Intelligence and Analysis perform "an independent study on the feasibility of creating a counter terrorism intelligence agency" (U.S. House of Representatives, 2006, p. 122). We were not asked to make a recommendation, and this assessment does not do so. Instead, it carefully lays out the relevant considerations for and the pros and cons of creating such an agency.

Concerns and Possible Responses

If America's counterterrorism-focused domestic intelligence, broadly conceived, is found wanting—and how to do better while preserving civil liberties is the policy challenge—changing organizations is one approach. But it is only one. Organizational approaches should be considered against a broader range of policy approaches—including spending more money, changing laws, and improving leadership or the means for sharing information. Our charge did not include detailed assessments of the performance of any U.S. agency. Instead, we consider whether reorganization could be expected to achieve significant improvements with regard to the concerns commonly expressed about the current U.S. arrangements for domestic intelligence, concerns which may or may not be valid in light of ongoing reforms in domestic intelligence undertaken since September 11.

Table S.1 lays out several concerns expressed about domestic intelligence in the United States—based on interviews, a panel of experts, and a review of literature—and, in the right-hand column, possible solutions, including reorganization, that would be relevant to that concern.

To take one example, if the FBI is dominated by a law enforcement and case-based approach, then creating a new intelligence organization would indeed be one possible solution. But, as Table S.1 indicates, a number of other approaches could also be relevant. Increasing

Table S.1
Expressed Concerns and Possible Responses

Expressed Concern	Possible Responses
If the FBI is dominated by a law enforcement and case-based approach; and if, as a result, collection is dominated by case requirements and analysis is dominated by operational support . . .	. . . then increase resources, change organization, change culture, change laws, change regulations or orders, and/or improve leadership.
If the FBI, CIA, and other agencies do not talk to each other . . .	. . . then change organization, change culture, change laws, change regulations or orders, enhance collaboration, and/or improve leadership.
If too much poor-quality information is collected, and collection efforts are too uncoordinated . . .	. . . then change regulations or orders, enhance collaboration, and/or improve leadership.
If analysis is fragmented and sometimes conflicting; and if the National Counterterrorism Center (NCTC), which acts as a central clearinghouse, mostly provides information to the President rather than to other intelligence organizations . . .	. . . then change organization, change regulations or orders, enhance collaboration, and/or improve leadership.
If it is difficult to move information and analysis across the domestic intelligence enterprise . . .	. . . then increase resources, change regulations or orders, enhance collaboration, and/or improve leadership.

resources might be necessary but not sufficient, since organizations tend to respond to more money by doing more of what they were already doing. In any event, the FBI's budget more than doubled between 2001 and 2008, from $3.1 billion to $6.4 billion.

Less dramatic organizational change could also be relevant. The Bureau created the National Security Branch to emphasize prevention and intelligence, particularly in the counterterrorism mission. That was part of an effort to transform culture in a number of ways, from recentralizing the management of terrorism cases, to training, to instituting a five-year "up or out" cap on supervisors to breed new leaders. Rapid growth means that more than half of FBI agents now have served for less than five years, presumably having joined an organization they did not perceive as dominated by traditional law enforcement. Changed laws, such as the PATRIOT Act, made it easier to collect counterterrorism intelligence, especially of the more exploratory sort, and changed regulations had the same effect, including dismantling the wall between intelligence and law enforcement.

Organizational Choices, Pros and Cons

Turning to the organizational dimension, "create a new domestic intelligence agency" can mean quite different things. This analysis focuses on the two most straightforward alternatives to the status quo, under which the FBI is charged with both domestic intelligence and law enforcement. The first alternative is to assemble parts of existing agencies to create a separate agency, one with a relationship to the Department of Justice similar to the one that the FBI already has. The second alternative is to create an "agency within an agency" in the FBI (or perhaps DHS).

If it remained at the FBI, the agency-within-an-agency would involve less short-term disruption than creating a stand-alone agency. How much it differed from what is being created in the FBI National Security Branch would be driven by decisions about how autonomous it should be in pursuing its intelligence mission. *Who* was recruited and *how* they were trained and rewarded would be matters of great consequence.

Because most public-sector organizations lack a handy bottom line, clarity in mission is critical, and that clarity provides a reason for thinking about a separate domestic intelligence agency. High-performing agencies begin with missions that are clear and clearly supported by Congress. For instance, the Social Security Administration's mission is to get checks and information to people who need them. By contrast, the Forest Service mission is split, to preserve public lands *and* produce resources from them.

Before its recent transformation, the FBI had a mission divided between law enforcement and intelligence. The question is whether a transformed FBI whose mission was intelligence-driven prevention would in fact have the clarity of a single mission. While law enforcement is a tool in prevention and can aid intelligence—if, for instance, the threat of prosecution helps recruit informants—the two remain quite different disciplines. The question is whether a transformed FBI whose mission was intelligence-driven prevention would in fact have the clarity of a single mission. Our assessment of other countries' domestic intelligence services suggested the value of a single focus, one that can foster what might be called a "culture of prevention" with respect to terrorism. Perhaps the single greatest teething pain of DHS—which brought together 180,000 employees from 22 existing agencies—has been that the constituent agencies did not share a single mission.

The other advantage of a separate service suggested by the review of other countries is that the new service might be able to draw on a wider, more diverse recruitment pool. The foreign services we reviewed feel that they are more able to attract individuals who would not normally be interested in entering a law enforcement profession, such as linguists, historians, social scientists, psychologists, economists and country/regional experts.

Yet the history of organizational design, and reorganization, in the public sector is cautionary in that it shows the process to be one of political competition among interests and interest groups. This helps explain why reorganizations in government so often seem to fail. If a new domestic intelligence service were created in "normal" circumstances—that is, not in the wake of another major attack—the result would be a political compromise and an agency that would likely not reflect exactly what any participant in the process sought.

The devil would be in the details, which would themselves be the result of compromises in the political arena. For instance, if the authorizing legislation were written in very specific terms, that would tie the hands of future officials in the organization—or insulate them from future pressures, depending on one's view of the outcome. The more independence a new agency had, the more autonomy it would have in shaping and sustaining its mission. If the new agency were located in some departmental hierarchy, it would surely matter which one: Being in the Department of Justice would make it part of an established organization dominated by law enforcement, whereas a location in DHS would subject it to the pressures of a work in progress, one now influenced by several forces, not the least of which are border control and crisis management.

Similarly, how many political appointees the agency had and whether they were appointed for fixed terms would also matter. The FBI is a very closed professional service, one dominated by its agents, with only a single political appointee—the director—and that appointee has a fixed, ten-year term. Until recently, lateral movements into the Bureau's senior managerial ranks were rare, and even now they are driven by needs for technical or management expertise, not politics. These considerations would all be important for a new agency, as would the height and width of the agency's hierarchy, the agency's latitude in selecting and training the professionals that would compose it, and a host of other details.

An Approach for Considering the Uncertain Costs and Benefits of Organizational Change

Some costs of a new agency, such as the basic organizational costs, are relatively tangible. As a benchmark, the portion of the FBI budget allocated to prevent terrorism and promote the nation's security, which includes both counterterrorism and counterintelligence activities, is $3.8 billion. In principle, if the entire National Security Branch, along with other government elements, were simply transferred to a new agency, the additional cost to the nation could be relatively small. There would still be, however, the costs of buildings and infrastructure (new data systems, new personnel systems and training, etc). Moreover, past experience suggests that while moving entire agencies is messy enough, attempts to move only parts are likely to be especially so. In this case, for instance, if the FBI-led Joint Terrorism Task Forces were transferred to a new agency, the FBI would have to duplicate the infrastructure, both physical and human, for reaching out to state and local authorities for law enforcement purposes. An "agency-within-an agency" likely would be cheaper, especially if it were built out of the National Security Branch. Yet it would still need new offices and infrastructure (new personnel systems, training facilities, and the like).

Other costs are more elusive—particularly the potential costs to privacy or civil liberties. On one hand, separating intelligence collection from law enforcement—that is, from the ability to act on that intelligence—could make a new service more acceptable to the public. Splitting the power to arrest and prosecute from intelligence efforts might be seen as safeguarding civil liberties. On the other hand, bounding intelligence by the pursuit of a specific criminal prosecution—the traditional law enforcement model as opposed to current FBI constraints—reduces the chance that individuals and groups will be watched long after they should have been dismissed as threats.

As that example illustrates, not only are data for judging performance in short supply and uncertainties large, many of the critical issues turn on values. In these circumstances, we applied a framework called "break-even analysis." This approach offers insight into how good a domestic intelligence agency would have to be, given a presumed level of threat and estimates of cost, to warrant creating it. It lets different people apply their own assessments and their own values.

Framing the risk of terrorist attacks in this approach is done in terms of the expected dollar cost of terrorism. As a starting point, estimates of the total cost of the September 11 terrorist attacks would suggest annual losses in the range of $1 billion to $10 billion—this is an average over time, with losses in any given year ranging from zero to much higher. We chose a wider range of average annual losses, from $100 million to $100 billion.

Figure S.1 maps the amount of threat reduction that a new arrangement for domestic intelligence would have to produce to justify creating it—to "break even"—given different costs and different assumptions about the level of risk the nation faces. For instance, if total domestic intelligence agency costs were estimated at $500 million annually, as shown in Figure S.1, then to break even the new service would have to reduce the nation's risk of terrorism by 50 percent if the annual risk were assumed to be $1 billion level, whereas it would only have to reduce the terrorism risk by 5 percent is that risk is assumed to be $10 billion.

What this analysis shows is that the choice turns on what level of terrorism risk is assessed or assumed, topics on which experts and

Figure S.1
Costs, Risks, and Risk Reduction for New Domestic Intelligence Arrangements

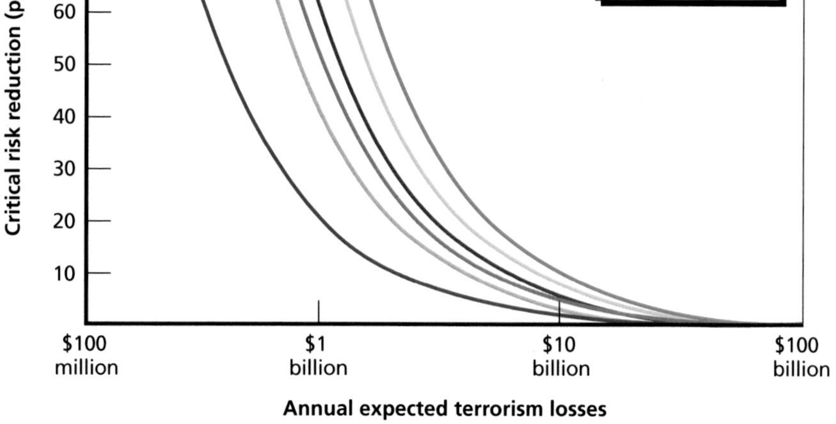

RAND *MG767-S.1*

policymakers differ considerably. For instance, assuming expected annual losses from terrorism of $100 billion per year, even a modestly effective agency can be justified at relatively high absolute cost. In principle, effects on privacy and civil liberties should be determined by the *mission and rules* governing collection, storage, and sharing of information, not on the *design* of the organization doing the collecting and storing. Yet it seems reasonable to assume that creating a new agency would imply that the nation sought more, and perhaps more intrusively collected, domestic intelligence. Otherwise, why do it? As a result, these intangible costs should be considered in any decision on structuring a domestic intelligence agency.

The results presented here are more a framework for policy debate than an answer to a specific policy question. The break-even framework presented here requires addressing the full range of costs and benefits of a policy choice in a common way. If people debating intelligence policy and the desirability of creating a new domestic intelligence agency disagree, this framework provides a systematic way to identify why they disagree. Do they differ on the terrorist risk, on the likely effectiveness of a reorganized domestic intelligence effort, or on how to protect civil liberties? Recognizing and addressing source of difference will, we hope, lead to a more productive debate than a simple fight over final conclusions.

The underlying message of this report is one of caution and deliberation. In an area in which metrics for direct assessment are limited and questions of values loom large, it is critical to consider carefully the implications and potential outcomes of significant policy changes. That is all the more so in this case, when creating a new organization or sharply reorganizing an existing one would have reverberations on existing efforts across a web of institutions and people at many levels inside and outside government.

Acknowledgments

A study as broad as this one is truly a group project, with debts aplenty to acknowledge, and I happily do so. Brian Jackson, as project co-leader, drove the project from the beginning, and he did the lion's share of the drafting, especially early on. The panel of experts that RAND assembled took time from their very busy schedules to assess domestic intelligence arrangements and approaches; they are listed in Appendix A, but we especially appreciate their service to their country, as well as that of the other experts we interviewed. Some colleagues who wrote particular background papers are thanked in this text, and, in many cases, their work is published in the companion volume to this report. But we want to acknowledge them all here as well: Anthony Butera, Peter Chalk, Lindsay Clutterbuck, Ben Goldsmith, Jeremiah Goulka, David Howell, Gordon Lee, Genevieve Lester, Martin Libicki, Darcy Noricks, Jack Riley, Agnes Schaefer, Douglas Shontz, Richard Warnes, and Michael Wermuth. We particularly note the contributions of our RAND colleagues Lynn Scott, Michael Hix, Andrew Morral, Kathi Webb, John Parachini, and Jerry Sollinger, as well as Jim Bruce and Charlie Nemfakos, who devoted considerable effort both in review and discussion sessions to keep us on track. The contributions of our three reviewers, Paul Light, Daniel Byman, and Paul Pillar, were thoughtful and demanding, and they much improved this document. Needless to say, though, we alone remain responsible for any gremlins that remain.

Abbreviations

9/11 Commission	National Commission on Terrorist Attacks on the United States
AFP	Australian Federal Police
ASIO	Australian Security Intelligence Organisation
ATAC	Anti-Terrorism Advisory Council
BfV	Bundesamt für Verfassungsschutz (German)
Bureau	Federal Bureau of Investigation
CBO	Congressional Budget Office
CBP	Customs and Border Protection
Church Committee	U.S. Senate Select Committee to Study Governmental Operations with Respect to Intelligence Activities
CIA	Central Intelligence Agency
CIFA	Counterintelligence Field Activity
CSIS	Canadian Security Intelligence Service
DCI	Director of Central Intelligence
DHS	Department of Homeland Security
DNI	Director of National Intelligence
DST	Direction de la Surveillance du Territoire (French)

EOUSA	Executive Office for United States Attorneys
FBI	Federal Bureau of Investigation
FEMA	Federal Emergency Management Agency
FISA	Foreign Intelligence Surveillance Act
FISC	Foreign Intelligence Surveillance Court
FTTTF	Foreign Terrorist Tracking Task Force
GIGN	Gendarmerie Nationale (French)
Gilmore Commission	Advisory Panel to Assess Domestic Response Capabilities for Terrorism Involving Weapons of Mass Destruction
HSAS	Homeland Security Advisory System
HSIN	Homeland Security Information Network
IG	Inspector General (French)
ISE	Information Sharing Environment
JITF-CT	Joint Intelligence Task Force for Combating Terrorism
JTTF	Joint Terrorism Task Force
LfV	Landesamt für Verfassungsschutz (German)
NADIS	Nachrichtendienstlichen Informationssystem (German)
NCTC	National Counterterrorism Center
NIC	National Intelligence Council
NIC-C	National Intelligence Coordination Center
NJTTF	National Joint Terrorism Task Force
NSA	National Security Agency
NSB	National Security Branch (of the Federal Bureau of Investigation)

OIA	Office of Intelligence and Analysis (in the Department of Homeland Security)
PSEP	Minister of Public Safety and Emergency Preparedness (Canadian)
RCMP	Royal Canadian Mounted Police
RG	Renseignements Generaux (French)
SAR	Suspicious Activity Report
SET	Strategic Execution Team
SIRC	Security and Intelligence Review Committee (Australian)
USAO	United States Attorney's Office
USA PATRIOT Act	Uniting and Strengthening America by Providing Appropriate Tools Required to Intercept and Obstruct Terrorism Act
WMD	weapons of mass destruction
WMD Commission	Commission on the Intelligence Capabilities of the United States Regarding Weapons of Mass Destruction

CHAPTER ONE

Introduction: Domestic Intelligence in Context

The terrorist threat to the United States varies in both form and source. Part of the threat comes from abroad, in the form of plots hatched overseas by foreign nationals who then come to the United States to finish their preparations and execute their plans, as was the case with the September 11 attacks. Terrorist threats can also develop within a country's borders. This was the case with the bombing attacks on London's public transport system on July 7, 2005, and a number of plots have been identified and disrupted inside the United States as well. Beyond the current focus on terrorist threats inspired by radical Islam and associated with al Qaeda and Osama bin Laden, the United States has long faced other terrorist threats. Until September 2001, the 1995 attack on the Murrah Federal Building in Oklahoma City was one of the most serious domestic terrorist attacks in U.S. history. Groups with various ideologies and agendas—such as radical right-wing, racist, or environmental groups—have also occasionally engaged in violent or destructive actions. Though the level of threat such groups currently pose may differ widely from that posed by groups seeking to stage repeated mass-casualty attacks, all are part of the overall terrorist threat that the United States faces.

The shadow of September 11 looms large over the continuing effort to prevent future terrorist attacks on the United States. Although more Americans have been killed by lightning than by terrorism since September 11,[1] the scale of the September 11 attacks was unprecedented

[1] In 2005, for instance, the numbers were 56 for terrorism versus an average of 62 per year for lightning over the previous five years. See U.S. Department of State, Office of the Coordinator for Counterterrorism (2006).

in America's experience with terrorism, and they stand as a permanent reminder of what can happen if the nation's guard is down. The September 11 attacks represented failure on many dimensions: the failure of airport security first and foremost, but also a failure of intelligence. This intelligence failure was not only one of imagination but also of warning: The signs of an impending attack were not assembled into a tactical warning that might have made it possible to prevent the disaster.

In the attacks' wake, a key question in the fight against terrorism is whether the United States needs a dedicated domestic intelligence agency separate from law enforcement, on the model of many U.S. allies and friends.[2] Though September 11 and the perceived failures that preceded it have framed the debate surrounding domestic intelligence and the need for a new domestic intelligence agency, such an agency would have to address the full range of terrorist threats that the United States faces and recognize how they have evolved since 2001.

To examine these issues, Congress directed that the Department of Homeland Security (DHS) Office of Intelligence and Analysis perform "an independent study on the feasibility of creating a counter terrorism intelligence agency" (U.S. House of Representatives, 2006, p. 122). DHS turned to RAND to conduct this study.

RAND was not asked to make a definitive judgment about whether a separate agency is wise policy, and this analysis does not do so. Rather, it seeks to frame the policy choices. We develop this framework by considering concerns that have been raised about current domestic intelligence arrangements, and then assessing whether any of these concerns might be ameliorated by reorganization. That does not imply that the concerns identified, many of which were first formulated in the immediate aftermath of September 11, are necessarily valid.

---

[2] See, for example, discussion in Advisory Panel to Assess Domestic Response Capabilities for Terrorism Involving Weapons of Mass Destruction (2002, p. iii–iv; hereafter referred to as the Gilmore Commission); Deutch (2003); Martin (2004); Posner (2006, pp. 121–139); Crumpton (2005, p. 210); Hamre (2003); Commission on the Intelligence Capabilities of the United States Regarding Weapons of Mass Destruction (2005, p. 451), Carter, Deutch, and Zelikow (1998, p. 80), Markle Foundation Task Force (2003); Markle Foundation Task Force (2002, p. 2); and Masse, O'Neil, and Rollins (2007, p. 11), which vary in how they envision such an agency being constituted.

Framing the Question

Information on intelligence issues—such as how, and how well, intelligence agencies perform—is in short supply, in large part because of the requirements that such activities be secret. Metrics are also elusive because the goal of counterterrorism is *nothing,* no attack. However, if none ensues—as has been the case in the United States since September 11—have the nation's counterterrorism efforts been effective or simply lucky, or was the threat overstated? In the absence of attacks, some measures are available to assess the performance of current counterterrorism efforts, such as disrupted plots and the details of how they were disrupted, but again, much of that information is hidden in secrecy. Moreover, we cannot know how many—if any—potential adversaries decided not to attack at all as a result of preventive or preparedness measures put in place to deter them.

Successful prevention of domestic terrorism depends on the integration of capabilities residing in intelligence and law enforcement organizations. Although the United States does not currently have a dedicated domestic intelligence agency devoted to counterterrorism, many efforts to detect and prevent domestic terrorist attacks are underway. Shortcomings in the effectiveness or acceptability of these efforts would be the most persuasive rationale for a major change in intelligence policy. Specifically, the argument for creating a new agency must rest on the belief that doing so would improve the nation's ability to detect and prevent terrorism. The magnitude of that assumed improvement defines the potential benefit of the shift in policy and the cost we should be willing to pay to achieve those benefits.

If America's counterterrorism-focused domestic intelligence, broadly conceived, is found wanting—and how to do better while preserving civil liberties is the policy issue—changing organizations is one approach.[3] But it is only one. Congress has many other approaches

---

[3] Indeed, other analysts have pointed out that several fundamental policy questions about the goals and appropriate activities of U.S. domestic intelligence efforts have not been answered. These questions must be addressed before or as part of any consideration of major structural reorganization activities. Heyman (2000) points out that an overarching framework specifying what the United States is seeking to accomplish through domestic intel-

available to improve domestic intelligence: Resources can be increased or reallocated across activities; the missions and priorities of existing organizations can be adjusted; laws, regulations and policies can be changed; personnel can be retrained and those with new skills hired; and new technologies or processes can be employed. The choice of approach depends on the problem being addressed.

Moreover, any actions taken to improve domestic intelligence must take into consideration not only actual effects on privacy and civil liberties but also the public's perception of those effects. Carefully crafted policies may allow for improvements in domestic intelligence capabilities without corresponding reductions in civil liberties,[4] but there is a tendency to view these choices within the context of a zero-sum game. Policies perceived as invasive by the public may be rejected, independent of their actual effects in individual privacy or liberty.

Finally, domestic intelligence activities aimed at identifying and preventing terrorist plots *before* the would-be terrorists can act are one part of the overall national effort, and should be seen in that context. The national effort ranges from action taken in other countries to attack foreign terrorist groups directly to broad efforts to deter and influence individual group members or the groups' sympathizers.[5] Seen in that light, success in one area—for example, foreign intelligence operations targeting terrorist groups abroad—may abet success in others and may also affect the demand for other elements of counterterrorism.

Research Approach

The question posed to the RAND team was organizational, but from the start it seemed important to embed that specific issue not only in

---

ligence and, subsequently, how that should shape government domestic intelligence initiatives, is largely missing.

4 See, for example, discussion in Halperin (1975–1976) for a more traditional framing of the issue or Taipale (2004–2005), which questions extensively the idea of a tradeoff between security and liberty.

5 Regarding deterrence and influence in counterterrorism, see Davis and Jenkins (2002), Stevenson (2004), National Research Council (2002), and Carter (2001).

the wider context of issues in domestic intelligence—many of which are not primarily organizational—but also to frame it against a broader discussion of exactly what problems with domestic intelligence were thought to need addressing. Accordingly, the study team took a number of perspectives in framing the issue in these broader terms:

- Through **historical analysis,** the team mined the nation's long and controversial history with domestic intelligence for insight that could inform future choices about arrangements for domestic intelligence.
- The team's **examination of current domestic intelligence efforts** reviewed available information about the structure of current efforts and perceived problems with intelligence activities.
- The team made an **assessment of the societal context**, examining available data and approaches for understanding the potential acceptability of a new intelligence agency in the United States.
- The researchers performed **legal analysis**, studying the legal and regulatory frameworks that define the scope of intelligence activities in the United States—though many of the legal issues do not turn on whether or not the nation creates a new intelligence agency.
- The researchers used **comparative case studies** to examine the experiences of six comparable democracies, all but one of which have a separate domestic intelligence agency.
- The researchers mined **organization theory** for insights about how to change organizations and their cultures and how to match policy choices to objectives.
- Finally, **interaction with a range of experts on and practitioners from law enforcement and domestic intelligence agencies** provided assessments of current and potential future intelligence arrangements.

The History of U.S. Domestic Intelligence

Gathering intelligence at home is as old as the Republic. It was, however, the twentieth century that saw domestic intelligence increasingly formalized in government institutions and that also witnessed several cycles of what was perceived as excessive zealousness followed by retrenchment. The Alien and Sedition Acts were passed in 1798 in response to concerns that social upheaval like that seen in the French Revolution would occur in the United States. The Secret Service, which had been established to investigate counterfeiting, took on domestic intelligence functions in the Spanish-American War. The Department of Justice (DOJ) later established the Bureau of Investigation to address interstate crime problems, and the Bureau took on the domestic intelligence mission during World War I because the military did not have the resources to do it. J. Edgar Hoover joined the Bureau in 1917, working under Attorney General A. Mitchell Palmer to investigate suspected anarchists and terrorists. In the years between World Wars I and II, the Bureau of Investigation was renamed the Federal Bureau of Investigation (FBI), cementing its identity as a federal law enforcement agency.

Over time, domestic intelligence activities broadened in scope and effect. Intelligence activities after World War I led to the 1920 "Palmer Raids" and the detention of some 10,000 suspected Communists and Communist Labor Party members in 33 cities. In later years, as the definition of threats broadened and the range of people subject to domestic intelligence attention increased, the FBI built lists of people labeled as Communists, subversives, and threats of other kinds. Through the 1940s and 1950s, the Bureau began infiltrating domestic organizations, beginning with Communist groups, hate groups, civil rights groups, and antiwar organizations.

Efforts to scale back such activities had limited effect, because the Bureau did not destroy the various lists when it was directed to do so. Files on individuals accumulated at FBI headquarters, and other agencies—the Central Intelligence Agency (CIA), National Security Agency (NSA), and Army intelligence—became engaged in domestic intelligence activities. The justification and ostensible target of the

FBI "counterintelligence programs"—COINTELPRO as the Bureau labeled it—was the suspected operations of hostile foreign intelligence services and especially their possible involvement in protests against the war in Vietnam.[6] But most of COINTELPRO's specific targets were American citizens in civil rights and antiwar groups, reflecting the broadening view in the programs of what constituted a threat to U.S. stability. People such as Reverend Martin Luther King were not only watched but also harassed, and worse.[7]

In their time, the Alien and Sedition Acts and Palmer Raids after World War I eventually came to be perceived as abuses of power; in the 1970s, the nation reacted similarly to the post–World War II expansion of domestic intelligence. That reaction took the form of the first-ever congressional investigations of intelligence: The Church Committee in the Senate and the Pike Committee in the House, so named after their chairs, Senator Frank Church and Representative Otis Pike. Those investigations and their aftermath set the context for domestic intelligence in the United States until September 11.[8] The committees concluded that organizations across government that had been given the powers to carry out domestic intelligence out of initial concern about the threat of Communism in the post-war period had, in an environment of lax oversight, political influences, and poor framing of their acceptable missions and activities, used those powers inappropriately and in some cases illegally. In reaction to the revelations, the nation judged that the Communist threat at home no longer justified intru-

---

6 See *Final Report of the Select Committee to Study Governmental Operations with Respect to Intelligence Activities of the United States Senate*, 94th Congress, 2nd Session, 1976, Book II, *Intelligence Activities and the Rights of Americans*, and Book III, *Supplementary Detailed Staff Reports on Intelligence Activities and the Rights of Americans*. For links to these reports, as well as to a rich range of other documents, both historical and contemporary, see Wolf (no date).

7 Concerns about domestic intelligence activities, while frequently focused on the activities of federal level organizations during this period, existed at the state and local level as well. See, for example, Schertzing (1999) for a case study of domestic intelligence activities of a state police agency in the period from World War I through the Church Committee investigations of the 1970s.

8 See Schwarz (2007) for a recent reflection on relevant parallels between the issues faced by the committees and concerns of the present day.

sive surveillance of Americans, if it ever had. The domestic intelligence activities of the FBI were sharply restrained, and a "wall" separating intelligence from law enforcement was erected.[9]

A compromise between presidential discretion and civil liberties resulted in the passage, in 1978, of the Foreign Intelligence Surveillance Act (FISA; Public Law 95-511) and the creation of the Foreign Intelligence Surveillance Court (FISC), a court operating in secret to grant covert wiretap and other surveillance authority for intelligence—as opposed to law enforcement—purposes. Before FISC, presidents had claimed the right of searches for national security purposes with no warrants whatsoever—a claim to which President George W. Bush returned after September 11.

The "wall" between intelligence and law enforcement had effects all across both domains, and FISA made the divide explicit. If the FBI or other officials sought wiretaps or other surveillance for criminal cases, they had to submit Title III affidavits to federal courts, indicating the "probable cause" that the location or communication line being bugged had been or was being used to commit crimes. Potential future use did not count. If, by contrast, the purpose of the surveillance was national security, with no reasonable belief that a crime had yet been committed, then FISA mandated a chain of procedure that ran from the FBI to the Department of Justice to the FISC.

Following the attacks of September 11 and the subsequent report from the National Commission on Terrorist Attacks on the United States (also known as "the 9/11 Commission"),[10] portentous questions

---

[9] There have been concerns that the changes imposed in response to the revelations of misbehavior significantly reduced the ability of the country to fight terrorism. For example, in the 1980s RAND carried out a research effort specifically examining the effect of the post–Church Committee restrictions on the ability to prevent terrorist activity and prosecute terrorism-related offenses (Wildhorn, Jenkins, and Lavin, 1982). The RAND team concluded that the change did not significantly affect prosecution success but did affect preventive intelligence action.

[10] National Commission on Terrorist Attacks on the United States (2004c; hereafter referred to as the 9/11 Commission). The 9/11 Commission was charged with preparing "a full and complete account of the circumstances surrounding the September 11, 2001, terrorist attacks" and asked to "provide recommendations designed to guard against future attacks."

were raised about domestic intelligence and counterterrorism efforts, and a number of changes were proposed to help prevent future terrorist attacks.[11] In response, many law enforcement and intelligence activities shifted focus. The first and perhaps most important development was the creation of DHS, which was founded in 2002 and began operations in 2003, combining activities that previously had been scattered across a number of agencies and initiating new intelligence and other programs aimed at preventing terrorism. Second, the FBI moved to transform its primary mission from law enforcement to counterterrorism intelligence and prevention. To reflect this new focus, the FBI created an office of intelligence and then, on the recommendation of the Commission on the Intelligence Capabilities of the United States Regarding Weapons of Mass Destruction (the "WMD Commission"),[12] merged that office with its Counterterrorism and Counterintelligence Divisions to form a new National Security Branch (NSB). The FBI has also worked to upgrade the status of intelligence within the organization, by creating Field Intelligence Groups (FIGs) in all 56 of its field offices, by elevating the status of intelligence analysts within the organization, and by creating an intelligence career track (one of five) for special agents.[13] Associated with these changes was a doubling in the size of the FBI to 12,000 agents and 30,000 employees, and a substantial expansion of its overseas presence through its legal attachés, which now have offices in more than 70 foreign cities

In August 2004, the National Counterterrorism Center (NCTC)[14] was established as the coordinator at the federal level for terrorism information and assessment, and in December 2004, the position of Director of National Intelligence (DNI) was created to provide strategic management (i.e., allocate resources, facilitate coordinated activity,

---

[11] As we will discuss later, the 9/11 Commission did not recommend creation of a new domestic intelligence agency, although it was considered in the group's deliberations.

[12] Commission on the Intelligence Capabilities of the United States Regarding Weapons of Mass Destruction (2005, p. 451; hereafter referred to as the WMD Commission).

[13] To be sure, the upgrading of intelligence analysts has not been without its challenges. See DOJ OIG (2007b).

[14] See National Counterterrorism Center (no date).

and promote information sharing) across the 16 intelligence agencies.[15] New legal authorities accompanied these organizational changes, especially the Uniting and Strengthening America by Providing Appropriate Tools Required to Intercept and Obstruct Terrorism Act (USA PATRIOT Act; P. L. 107-56), which significantly broadened the ability of federal government organizations to collect and share intelligence information domestically.

At the state and local level, government organizations have reorganized around the counterterrorism and homeland security missions, and resources have been shifted to detecting and preventing terrorist attacks.[16] Initiatives to improve collaboration across the federal system, such as the FBI-led Joint Terrorism Task Forces (JTTFs), have been expanded—between 2001 and 2007, the number of JTTFs across the country grew from 34 to over 100—and new ones, such as DHS's fusion centers, have been put in place (Masse, O'Neil, and Rollins, 2007).[17]

These shifts have largely removed the "wall" that had existed between intelligence and law enforcement activities[18] and have increased

15 The legislation making these changes was the Intelligence Reform and Terrorism Prevention Act of 2004 (P. L. 108-458).

16 See, for example, Riley et al. (2005) and Marks and Sun (2007).

17 The focus of JTTFs is cases and investigations, though now the cases themselves are collection platforms. One key JTTF function is "deconflicting" investigations—that is, parceling out cases to JTTF member agencies for their investigations, then making sure that the investigations don't work at cross purposes to one another. The newer "fusion centers," a DHS initiative, are meant to complement JTTFs by assembling *strategic intelligence* at the regional level. They, too, seek to bring together federal with state and local officials, including, in principle, reaching out to the private sector.

18 According to the 9/11 Commission (2004a, pp. 4–5):

> Certain provisions of federal law had been interpreted to limit communication between agents conducting intelligence investigations and the criminal prosecution units of the Department of Justice. This was done so that the broad powers for gathering intelligence would not be seized upon by prosecutors trying to make a criminal case. The separation of intelligence from criminal investigations became known as the "wall." New procedures issued by Attorney General Reno in 1995 required the FBI to notify prosecutors when "facts and circumstances are developed" in a foreign intelligence or foreign counterintelligence investigation that "reasonably indicate a significant federal crime has been, is being, or may be committed." The procedures, however, prohibited the

the number of organizations that are involved in monitoring what is going on inside the country, assessing possible threats, and acting to disrupt potential terrorist activity.[19]

The controversial history of U.S. domestic intelligence activities suggests a range of lessons relevant to considering major changes in current intelligence efforts. However effective government organizations are at collecting and using domestic intelligence, if they are not specifically tasked and overseen, the focus of intelligence activities can drift from a specific threat to broader views of what might be destabilizing to the nation. That, in turn, creates a risk that individuals will become targets of government attention because of mere dissent, rather than the potential for violence.

History also shows that the public's acceptance of domestic intelligence activities is imperative, and that what is considered acceptable can both be fragile and shift significantly over time. Views similarly vary among individuals. Public demand for domestic intelligence is driven by the perceived threat it is intended to address, and those perceptions can change much more rapidly than the threat itself.[20] For instance, polls taken immediately after the September 11 attacks asking how concerned respondents were about more terrorist attacks in the United States recorded 49 percent as worrying "a great deal" and 38 percent

---

prosecutors from "directing or controlling" the intelligence investigation. Over time, the wall requirement came to be interpreted by the Justice Department, and particularly the Foreign Intelligence Surveillance Court, as imposing an increasingly stringent barrier to communications between FBI intelligence agents and criminal prosecutors. Despite additional guidance on information sharing issued by Attorney General Reno in February 2000 and by Deputy Attorney General Larry Thompson in August 2001, the wall remained a source of considerable frustration and concern within the Justice Department.

19 Some question using the metaphor of a single wall to describe the multiple barriers that existed to restrict intelligence activity domestically: "There was never just one wall. . . . Some walls were meant to protect individual rights. Others were meant to protect national security interests. . . . [Post–September 11th legislation] broke down the walls indiscriminately, scarcely considering what purpose they served and never asking what should replace them to guide both law enforcement and intelligence agencies" (Berman and Flint, 2003, p. 56).

20 Among many studies focusing on aspects of these attributes, see Fischoff et al. (2003), Huddy (2005), Davis and Silver (2004), and Sunstein (2003).

worrying "somewhat." Two years later, the proportion worrying "a great deal" had fallen to 25 percent, whereas the percentage reporting that they were "somewhat" concerned had risen to 46.[21] However, polling cannot really capture in detail what people seek from intelligence activities.[22] Moreover, changes in the law and in government organization and practice are not rapid, and it is unlikely that the practice of intelligence will—or should—adapt to the pendulum swings in public attitudes. The public also reserves the right to pass retrospective judgment about perceived oversteps, failings, or improper behavior by intelligence organizations after the fact, and those judgments can lead to sharp restrictions in domestic intelligence operations.

This dynamic in public attitudes has been clear in the responses to the host of changes in domestic intelligence policy since September 11. The list includes the changes in intelligence practices and authorities included in the USA PATRIOT Act, domestic wiretapping and intercept activities by the NSA, revisions to the Attorney General's guidelines that govern investigative practices relating to terrorism, the involvement of U.S. military organizations in domestic intelligence activities, proposals for programs for broad citizen reporting of suspicious activity to the government, and the sharing and use of commercial and other databases between the government, private sector, and other actors for data mining and other counterterrorism analysis.

Many of these concerns are tangential to the specific organizational question to which this report is addressed. Yet they will surely be invoked in the debate about whether to create a separate domestic intelligence agency. They would also bear, if not on how a new agency was structured, then surely on what authorities it was given and how it was to conduct its business. These concerns would also affect how it related to the other elements of the nation's domestic intelligence enterprise—federal, state, local, and private sector.

---

21 For a compilation of polls, see two American Enterprise Institute for Public Policy Research studies, *America and the War on Terror* (2007) and *Public Opinion on the War with Iraq* (2008).

22 See, for example, Best and McDermott (2007).

How This Report Is Organized

Chapter Two describes what is meant by domestic intelligence. Chapter Three explores the possible and perceived problems with the current processes, and Chapter Four frames a number of possible policy approaches. Chapter Five turns in detail to the specific organizational question: What problems might a separate domestic intelligence agency address? Chapter Six looks at approaches to making a decision about the creation of a new agency in the absence of data. Chapter Seven presents conclusions and suggests a way forward. Members of the expert panel that the RAND team assembled are listed in Appendix A; Appendix B consists of a graphic representation of the RAND team's "mapping" of the current U.S. domestic intelligence enterprise.

CHAPTER TWO

Defining Domestic Intelligence

No consensus definition of domestic intelligence has been established in law or public policy (Masse, 2003 and 2006). Indeed, the absence of consistent definitions and a defined framework laying out what activities should be included in domestic intelligence and the range of goals domestic intelligence efforts are designed to achieve has been flagged as a major source of concerns about current activities (Heyman, 2007). We define domestic intelligence as follows:

> efforts by government organizations to gather, assess, and act (see Figure 2.1) on information about individuals or organizations in the United States or U.S. persons[1] elsewhere *that is not necessarily related to the investigation of a known past criminal act or specific planned criminal activity.*[2]

While the term *intelligence* originated in its association with the secret activities of governments advancing their interests in international affairs, it is used to mean many things, now all the more so when competitive intelligence has become a private-sector fashion. In recent years, use of the term *intelligence* has been integrated into domestic law enforcement and public safety agencies as "intelligence-led polic-

---

1 "Federal law and executive order define a U.S. Person as: a citizen of the United States, an alien lawfully admitted for permanent residence, an unincorporated association with a substantial number of members who are citizens of the U.S. or are aliens lawfully admitted for permanent residence, or a corporation that is incorporated in the U.S." (National Security Agency, no date).

2 For a historical discussion, see Morgan (1980, p. 13).

Figure 2.1
Three Core Functions of Domestic Intelligence

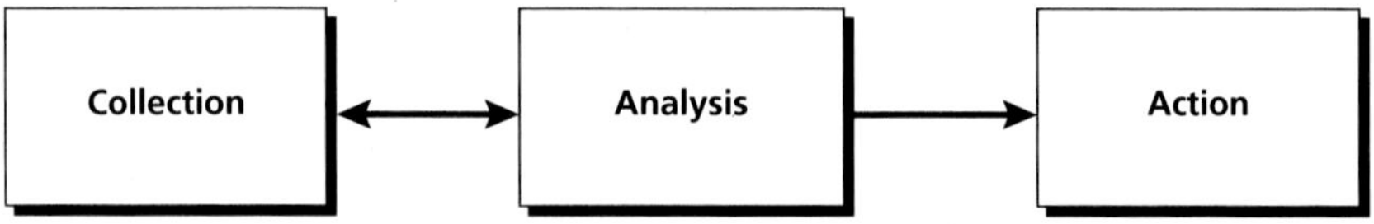

RAND *MG767-2.1*

ing." Definitions of *intelligence-led policing* vary, but common elements include the use of information-gathering capabilities and the analysis and application of that information in crime-prevention and -response activities, rather than only in the prosecution of specific past criminal acts.[3]

To be sure, terrorists are criminals—but many of them commit only one spectacular crime, and then it is too late for intelligence to matter. Furthermore, while our discussion focuses on terrorism, domestic intelligence is about more than the threat of terrorist attack. Counterintelligence aimed at detecting members or activities of foreign intelligence services and at understanding the broader activities of criminal organizations, such as drug cartels, criminal gangs, or money-laundering operations, may also involve collecting information not specifically related to individual criminal acts.[4]

Intelligence organizations work against terrorism by carrying out activities designed to detect the types of activities terrorist organizations or violent individuals acting alone would do before actually staging an attack. These activities include recruiting, training, acquiring logistics and resources (e.g., buying weapons), surveillance and reconnaissance of potential targets, planning efforts, and the early stages of operations, when they are initiated but before they are complete.[5]

---

[3] See, for example, discussion in Weisburd and Braga (2006), Milligan et al. (2006), Ratcliffe (2002), and Bureau of Justice Assistance, U.S. Department of Justice (2005).

[4] This broader view is included in our discussion of current U.S. domestic intelligence activities in the next chapter.

[5] For a recent RAND review of these steps in more detail, see Don et al. (2007).

Domestic intelligence activities can be divided into two overlapping categories—*investigation* and *exploration*. If, as occurred with the possible terrorist group rolled up in Fort Dix, New Jersey, in 2007,[6] a citizen calls the FBI to report suspicious behavior, the first decision is whether it merits following up; in most cases, that decision will be made in the local FBI-led JTTF. If the lead is viewed as promising, the ensuing investigation will resemble what would occur in response to a lead about everyday criminal activity or the existence of a previously unknown organized crime group; the investigations will seek to uncover who is involved and for what purpose. The main difference from a criminal investigation might be that the decision to apprehend the group would be affected by two competing goals: the need to move quickly for fear that the group might actually commit a terrorist act and the desire to "let the operation run" to gather additional intelligence and potentially identify other participants in the plot.

When to act against an identified terrorist plot has been a point of some controversy since September 11. Immediately after the attacks, when there was an unwillingness to risk any suspected terrorist plot coming to fruition, the FBI was initially criticized for acting "too quickly" against identified plots and settling for the filing of charges other than terrorism. Doing so was viewed as sacrificing potential intelligence-gathering opportunities, where identified individuals might identify other yet unknown conspirators. The Bureau has changed its approach in recent years.[7] That change was described by a range of project interviewees. However, across different organizations, interviewees reported that different agencies within the domestic intelligence system differ in their approaches to the decision of when to act against monitored individuals or organizations.

From a purely law enforcement perspective, if a lead is not deemed worth following, that is the end of the matter. For intelligence pur-

---

[6] The Fort Dix plot allegedly involved six individuals who planned to attack the base using a variety of military-style assault weapons and was identified through a report by a clerk at a local video store who saw a video one of the men brought in to be duplicated that contained footage of weapons training and other suspicious activity (see "Official: Radicals Wanted to Create Carnage at Fort Dix," 2007).

[7] See discussion of both the original policy and the more recent shifts in Block (2007).

poses, however, it might become a piece of information to be tucked away to see whether it is repeated or forms part of a later pattern. That is perhaps the sharpest difference between case-based law enforcement investigations and intelligence investigations. A traditional case-based approach to law enforcement investigation closes off alternative lines of analysis. Once a decision was made to go to trial, information that might emerge contradicting the theory of prosecution would not be ignored, but resources would no longer be devoted to a wide-ranging or exploratory investigation of the crime. The emphasis would be on seeking evidence to confirm one hypothesis ("Fred killed Jack") and not on seeking information to confirm alternatives ("Mary is the killer," or "Jack killed himself"). Intelligence, in contrast, constantly seeks different information to undermine, as well as to confirm, its preferred approaches. It is also eager to revisit past assumptions.

Moreover, a case-based investigation does not freely share information *internally*, for much of what is collected—and discussed in wide-ranging grand jury proceedings—is extraneous to the case and inappropriate to share (for instance, that suspect X, who was later cleared of any wrongdoing, was cheating on his wife). For counterterrorism, by contrast, much of the information that might not be relevant to a particular conviction should be "in the system" and retrievable, say, ten years later if information makes important what earlier was not—for instance, that suspect X had a link to Y, who at the time was not important.

The *exploration* component of domestic intelligence also differs from law enforcement and includes two elements: information-gathering efforts in search of new leads and a broader warning function that requires building a wider understanding of the domestic threat environment. The first element involves broader data gathering about a greater number of individuals and organizations in an effort to proactively identify individuals or groups that might be planning violent actions. The second seeks to assemble a mosaic of understanding rather than to unravel a specific crime. On the collection side, both these elements could cover a wide range, from simply watching (post–September 11 changes permitted, for instance, FBI agents to observe at public houses of worship), to talking with local communities. Undercover agents might infiltrate particular groups of interest, as much to understand their motivations and actions as to uncover law breaking. Or an NSA analyst might transcribe a suspicious conversation between an American citizen and foreign national residing abroad. On the analytic side, the search for patterns could take many forms, from assembling information against hypotheses, to mining lots of data for patterns or connections,[8] to doing "network" analysis to understand particular groups. The point is to build understanding and, with luck, to uncover what it is we *don't* know. It is also to assess and anticipate the nature of the threat based on information, such as the experience of other countries with terrorism.

The warning function may not be able to identify specific plots or attacks, but its goal is to enable actions to be taken to respond to a change in the threat environment. Knowledge that groups are turning their sights on particular types of targets or increasing their activities can enable stepped-up prevention efforts in an effort to derail terrorists' activities even in the absence of specific tactical warning. In this sense, if much of investigation is puzzle solving, then warning is addressing mysteries.[9] Puzzles are issues that could be answered with certainty if only we had information that is, in principle, available. Once a crime is committed, investigating who did it is a matter of solving a puzzle. There *is* an answer.

In contrast, mysteries are future and contingent; no information is available to solve them with certainty. Much of exploratory analysis is framing mysteries, for the new plots and plotters uncovered may not be far along. Terrorists are the ultimate asymmetric threat; they shape their threat to our vulnerabilities. As a result, if warning is good enough at framing the mystery, that may induce Americans to act—for instance, stepping up inspections at vulnerable facilities—thus preventing the attacks, or at least causing terrorists to start planning all over again. Analogies to this sort of response to strategic warning exist in other areas, such as individuals buying stronger locks, bars for their windows, or security systems in response to an increase in the

---

8 See, for example, discussion in DeRosa (2004).

9 On the distinction between puzzles and mysteries, see Treverton (1994) and Nye (1994).

crime *rate*, rather than any *specific* threat to their home. In the realm of counterterrorism, an example of a general warning might be the use of the color-coded Homeland Security Advisory System (HSAS) that is designed to convey strategic level warning to the nation about the terrorist threat, whereas other warnings are more specific, such as the national warnings in 2004 that were directed at financial institutions in New York, northern New Jersey and Washington, D.C.

Such efforts demonstrate the challenges associated with effective use of such intelligence-generated warning in the domestic context: Changing protective measures in response to a perceived change in threat has real costs (e.g., personnel overtime to provide heightened security when the HSAS is changed from yellow to orange) and the less specific the warning, the higher those costs can be. This can make it challenging both to take action based on warning and to sustain the willingness to do so across the country over time.[10]

As our definition of domestic intelligence makes clear, many of the actions that could be involved are very sensitive, such as infiltrating groups and sifting through individuals' personal information. If the goal of counterterrorism efforts is to prevent acts of terrorism in America while protecting American civil liberties as expressed not just in the constitution but also in laws and practices, then how must those considerations shape the organizational structure and practices used in domestic intelligence efforts? To provide a foundation for that discussion, the next chapter describes current domestic intelligence arrangements and concerns about their effectiveness and acceptability.

---

10 For an overview of these issues, focused specifically on the HSAS, see Reese (2003).

CHAPTER THREE

Current Domestic Intelligence Arrangements and Their Performance

The central policy rationale for making major changes in domestic intelligence activities would be to correct perceived shortcomings in the way these functions and missions are currently being pursued. This chapter reviews the structure of current domestic intelligence arrangements, concerns about current capabilities, and the implications of intelligence efforts for civil liberties. Much of what follows does not speak directly to the organizational issue at hand but is being addressed so as to place that issue in the larger context of domestic intelligence performance more generally.

The Structure of Current Domestic Intelligence Efforts

To provide a basis for considering ways that domestic intelligence efforts might be restructured, RAND built a map of domestic intelligence activities at all levels, involving both governmental and nongovernmental organizations. The basis for the mapping effort was a review of open-source literature on current efforts to collect, analyze, and share information inside the United States.[1] Reflecting the fact that domestic

1 Sources of information for this review included published programmatic descriptions of intelligence and law enforcement organizations, analyses of government activities by internal executive branch offices (e.g., Inspectors General), legislative branch organizations (e.g., the Government Accountability Office, Congressional Budget Office), nongovernmental organizations, and the press.

intelligence activities involve more than terrorism, the mapping effort included efforts to control the smuggling of illegal drugs, law enforcement activities focused on controlling money laundering, and even information systems and activities associated with information-sharing and "intelligence-led" elements of traditional law enforcement.

The goal was to catalog, as comprehensively as possible, programs, initiatives, and activities and the cooperative or information-sharing linkages that existed between them to map the topography of the current domestic intelligence enterprise. The resulting mapping is included in Appendix B. While intended to be comprehensive, it was limited to those programs and initiatives that are overt or have been publicly disclosed.

If arrangements for domestic intelligence in the United States were considered an enterprise, what would be most obvious about it is that it is complex and dispersed. At the federal level, the role of the FBI is central, but other "three-letter agencies" also play a role. The CIA is enjoined from domestic activity, but transnational threats such as terrorism frustrate any tidy distinction. The sad saga of two of the September 11 hijackers, Khalid al-Mihdhar and Nawaf al-Hazmi, testifies to that fact. The CIA knew what the FBI did not: that the two were already resident in the United States in the summer of 2001.[2] The NSA is also enjoined from domestic spying, but the Bush administration judged that the threat after September 11 required it to monitor swatches of telephone calls from the United States abroad, including those made by American citizens.

The Department of Homeland Security, especially its Office of Intelligence and Analysis, has a variety of intelligence roles across intelligence functions. So do the Director of National Intelligence, the National Counterterrorism Center, and various military elements, given the nexus between information collected abroad for understanding domestic threats and military homeland defense missions. In addition, other agencies, such as the Coast Guard, the Drug Enforcement Administration, the Border Patrol, and the Transportation Security Administration (TSA), not only have large numbers of "embedded

---

2 9/11 Commission (2004c, pp. 268–272).

collectors"—staff members who might gather intelligence in the course of their day-to-day activities—they also are adjusting their operations to include counterterrorism. For instance, the Coast Guard's National Response Center's legacy mission focused on the reporting and response to hazardous-material incidents but now also includes reports of terrorist incidents (National Response Center, no date). A number of other federal organizations play smaller roles in the institutional context for domestic intelligence, as participants in activities spearheaded by others or in collecting and sharing intelligence information in specialized topical areas. This multilayer, dispersed organizational design is not surprising, as it mirrors the U.S. judicial system and reflects not only the history of domestic intelligence but also America's sense of invulnerability with respect to external attack. Much of this changed in the wake of September 11.

Beyond the federal level, the eyes and ears of domestic counterterrorism are the 18,000 units of government (including state and local) in the United States and the 700,000 sworn police officers (Riley et al., 2005). These sworn officers are augmented by private security guards, of whom there are three times as many as public law enforcement officers. Moreover, most of the "public" infrastructure in finance, transportation, information, and the like is in private hands, so those private-sector infrastructure managers are also on the front lines of the fight against terrorism. Several of the largest police departments—with New York in a class by itself—have large and sophisticated counterterrorism intelligence operations of their own. Most, though, have neither resources nor time for special intelligence gathering against terror. They can be eyes and ears in the course of their normal policing—*if* they know what to look for. The clash of organizational cultures is sharp enough at the federal level; it is only sharper across levels of the federal system.

The reality of the many players in domestic intelligence means that the structure of domestic intelligence efforts is a complex one, with interconnections among organizations at the federal, state, and local levels and outside government to the private sector and even the public.[3] Organizations such as JTTFs and fusion centers represent nodes in the network where many different entities interact, and information systems in the law enforcement and the homeland security communities provide bridges that information can flow across from one part of the enterprise to another.[4] Given the differences in organizational missions and the complex structure of domestic counterterrorism intelligence, what capabilities does this "enterprise" provide, and what are the concerns about these capabilities?

Domestic Intelligence: Capabilities and Concerns

Is the current domestic intelligence enterprise meeting the nation's counterterrorism needs? As alluded to earlier, it is difficult to reach solid conclusions about intelligence performance, particularly based on information that is available publicly. On the face, U.S. counterterrorism activities since September 11 have been successful—there have, as of mid-2008, been no major terrorist incidents domestically since then, and a number of plots (of admittedly varying levels of threat) have been identified and disrupted through intelligence activities. It is tempting to assume that the lack of attacks is the direct result of the activities that are in place to prevent them, but we cannot know for sure.

Data are scarce for assessing the functioning of individual components of the domestic intelligence effort: it is difficult to quantify the level of effort going into counterterrorism intelligence, as assets support multiple activities; the extent of the domestic terrorist threat is impos-

---

3 Our broad framing of the U.S. domestic intelligence enterprise resembles the framing of the "homeland security intelligence community" described in Masse (2006, pp. 21–23). The *DHS Intelligence Enterprise Strategic Plan* (DHS, 2006) uses the somewhat more general descriptive of the Homeland Security Stakeholder Community, of which the Homeland Security Intelligence Community consists of the subset of that group that have intelligence elements.

4 Though this study focuses on counterterrorism, a variety of other security and related missions involve domestic intelligence activities. For example, efforts to control the smuggling of illegal drugs into the country have long had associated intelligence efforts, and law enforcement activities focused on controlling money laundering involve significant financial intelligence infrastructures.

sible to know with any precision, so it is difficult to measure effectiveness against the threat; and the complexity of the domestic intelligence enterprise makes it difficult to determine how capable the country is overall at collecting, analyzing, and acting on intelligence information. These realities often lead assessors to focus on *inputs* (such as numbers of people assigned to the counterterrorism mission) and *outputs* (such as leads validated or intelligence reports produced) that, while informative, do not provide insight into whether the system is producing protective *outcomes*. They similarly do not provide insight into public perceptions of intelligence activities that drive the acceptability of current efforts.[5]

To help assess current efforts, RAND sought the input and views of a variety of individuals, including a panel of experts in intelligence policy and practitioners currently involved in domestic intelligence activities across government. The eight members of the expert panel are listed in Appendix A, while the individuals currently involved in domestic intelligence activities provided their input on a not-for-attribution basis. The goal in soliciting this input was to tap individuals both with a broader perspective on domestic intelligence activities, as well as those currently involved who would be in the best position to assess the strengths and weaknesses of current activities.

Among both the members of our expert panel and those interviewed over the course of the study, views varied dramatically about current domestic intelligence activities. In assessing current arrangements, the views of members of the expert panel clustered around the center of a scale from "very good" to "very poor," and they raised questions about the leadership of domestic intelligence efforts, how well suited current efforts are to the counterterrorism mission, and a variety of factors associated with the quality of the management and activities. Some expert panel participants (and interviewees as well) were particularly critical of the complex structure of the current domestic intelli-

5 For example: "The FBI has not developed performance measures for the NJTTF and FTTTF. Although the FBI has measures for the JTTFs as part of the field offices, many of the measures are output oriented rather than outcome oriented for the counterterrorism program" (DOJ OIG, 2005a, p. v).

gence enterprise, even at the federal level, let alone reaching out to the states and localities. One asserted that it has "no structure" and creates significant confusion for the domestic counterterrorism intelligence mission. Another described domestic intelligence as "a pickup ballgame without a real structure, leadership, management, or output."[6] However, the panel still gave current efforts at least some credit for significantly reducing the risk of terrorist attack in the United States since September 11.

Among interviewees within government, views varied considerably about whether current arrangements were effective or whether there were sufficient problems such that changes were necessary. Interviewees and panel members highlighted concerns that similar activities are proliferating at different places within the domestic intelligence system. Participants cited this as a result of confusion and ambiguity about the roles of particular agencies within the domestic intelligence enterprise and uncertainty about who is responsible for what parts of the effort. The fact that so many independent organizational actors, including those in the private sector, are involved inherently makes both an understanding of the capabilities of current domestic intelligence activities and any oversight of those activities challenging.

Although some practitioners we interviewed saw current intelligence efforts as meeting the nation's needs, the range of assessments—and the generally negative views among members of our panel of experts—suggest that there are substantial concerns about the functioning of the current intelligence system. Given the absence of data, we organized the expert views and the results of our literature review

---

[6] This judgment about domestic activities echoes public reporting of internal government consideration of the U.S. national counterterrorism effort overall:

> The counterterrorism infrastructure that resulted [from the expansion since September 11] has become so immense and unwieldy that many looking at it from the outside, and even some on the inside, have trouble understanding how it works or how much safer it has made the country. . . . Institutions historically charged with protecting the nation have produced a new generation of bureaucratic offspring—the Pentagon's Counterintelligence Field Activity (CIFA) and Joint Intelligence Task Force for Combating Terrorism (JITF-CT), the Treasury Department's Office of Intelligence and Analysis (OIA), and the FBI's National Security Service (NSS) [sic], to name a few—many with seemingly overlapping missions. (DeYoung, 2006, p. A1)

around the three elements of domestic intelligence—collection, analysis, and action. The result was several "expressed concerns" (Table 3.1) that sought to capture the range of concerns about the capabilities of current domestic intelligence efforts.

Collection

Broadly speaking, three sorts of concerns were identified about existing collection processes: (1) organizational biases against exploratory collection and retaining data; (2) poor coordination among domestic collection efforts; and (3) a large volume of data of questionable or poorly specified quality. Both types of intelligence collection, *investigative* and *exploratory*, may or may not relate to a known past or future criminal act. In its examination of U.S. counterterrorism efforts before the September 11 attacks, the 9/11 Commission described the focus of the efforts of the FBI—the central federal agency for domestic counterterrorism both then and now—as captive to a law enforcement approach to the problem. The Bureau focused its resources on "after-the-fact investigations of major terrorist attacks in order to develop criminal cases" (9/11 Commission, 2004a, p. 1). Agents were "trained to build cases, [and] developed information in support of their own cases, not as part of a broader more strategic [intelligence] effort" (9/11 Commission, 2004a, p. 3). Moreover, internal systems within the agency

Table 3.1
Concerns Expressed over Domestic Intelligence

Expressed Concern
The FBI is dominated by law enforcement and case-based approach. As a result, collection is dominated by case requirements and analysis is dominated by operational support.
The FBI, CIA, and other agencies do not talk to each other.
Too much poor-quality information is collected, and collection efforts are too uncoordinated.
Analysis is fragmented and sometimes conflicting; NCTC acts as a central clearinghouse, but it mostly provides information to the President rather than to other intelligence organizations.
It is difficult to move information and analysis across the domestic intelligence enterprise.

discouraged the use of tools such as FISA surveillance, the Attorney General's guidelines for terrorism investigations restricted the use of some sources of information, and concerns by individual agents about breaking the rules for domestic intelligence led to sharper self-imposed limits than the rules intended.

It remains a fair question how much the FBI has changed in these respects since September 11, despite its extensive transformation efforts. However, in both the literature and some of our interviews, this theme is extended to the broader claim that there are fundamental incompatibilities between the cultures of law enforcement and domestic intelligence. These differences are reinforced through training, regulations, authorities, incentives, and organizational culture. According to this line of argument, intelligence organizations view warning, and the actions it enables, as the product of their counterterrorism efforts, whereas law enforcement organizations view action, and especially prosecution, as the product of theirs. Authors such as Richard Posner (2006) and Stephen J. Schulhofer (2002) have suggested that even a substantially reorganized FBI, which has taken terrorism prevention as its top priority, cannot be expected to be successful given the vast differences between the disciplines of intelligence and law enforcement.[7]

However, that broad interpretation of the incompatibility between law enforcement and intelligence missions is disputed, for instance, in citing the growing prominence of intelligence-led policing and a focus on preventive operations in state and local law enforcement orga-

---

[7] According to Schulhofer (2002, p. 57):

> To expect a large, tradition-bound bureaucracy to quickly reorient its operations and change its fundamental culture is about as realistic as expecting the world's largest ocean liner to stop itself instantly and turn around on a dime. It might therefore make more sense to preserve the FBI as a primarily reactive, crime-solving agency and to build a new organization, perhaps a domestic equivalent of the CIA, to take charge of counterterrorism efforts.

See also the Gilmore Commission (2002, pp. iii). In fact, Paul Pillar (2004, p. 133) summarizes: "Whether to create such an agency in the United States is largely an issue of whether this mission should be left to the FBI."

nizations.[8] The FBI's transformation program is designed to make intelligence-led prevention drive all its programs, from counterterrorism to law enforcement. In this conception, cases become collection platforms, and enforcement is one tool in the prevention kitbag. Moreover, the history of domestic intelligence in the United States seems to caution against making too strong an assumption that the organization will be unable to be successful in doing intelligence. The Bureau's behavior in the 1950s and 60s led to the Church Committee review and ultimately the accusation of improprieties and imposed reform, but an inability to carry out domestic intelligence activities was not one of the bill of particulars levied against the FBI.[9]

Furthermore, some interviewees underscored the cost in effectiveness that might be imposed in separating intelligence from law enforcement—both because of the need to "hand off" cases to another agency to be acted upon[10] and because of the limits the separation might put on intelligence efforts by reducing access to information that could be produced during investigations of other criminal activity.

A different definition of the collection problem is that too many agencies are collecting information with too little coordination. While there can be benefits to decentralization and diversity in activity,[11] having many individual actors operating independently can create

---

8 For example:

> Instead of focusing on this truly difficult, yet essential, task of coordination, many have simply argued that there needs to be a shift from a law enforcement paradigm to an intelligence paradigm with a focus on preventing rather than solving crimes. This formulation, however, is based on faulty assumptions, and substitutes rhetoric for analysis. As the FBI points out, it has always been in the business of preventing terrorist attacks and it had some notable successes before September 11, such as the foiled plot to blow up the Holland Tunnel in New York in 1993. Rather than pose a falsely rigid dichotomy between law enforcement and intelligence, it is necessary to examine how intelligence information is actually used in counterterrorism. (Martin, 2004, p. 12)

9 See, for example, the comments of John MacGaffin in a 2003 *Frontline* interview ("Do We Need an MI5?" 2003).

10 This issue of needing to transfer intelligence across an organizational boundary to be acted upon was similarly evident in the international case studies done during this research effort.

11 See, for example, discussion in Posner (2006).

duplication and conflict. This question has arisen even within a single agency, such as the management and assessment of human sources in the various FBI Field Offices (9/11 Commission, 2004a, p. 7; WMD Commission, 2005, pp. 455–456). It has come up with regard to the collection practices in the intelligence elements of United States Attorney's offices.[12] Similar questions were raised during the internal DHS review about the potential for "multiple points of collection without coordination" within the Department's component agencies intelligence efforts.[13] Broadening from coordination of federal efforts to the domestic intelligence enterprise overall, state and local organizations have criticized the lack of a consolidated requirements process for homeland security intelligence to ensure that collection matches the needs of the relevant consumers (DHS, Lessons Learned Information Sharing System, 2005, p. 4). Bureaucratic conflict among organizations is also frequently cited as amplifying the coordination problems among government organizations at all levels of government.[14]

The third overarching concern about domestic collection activities is the quality of the information that is in fact collected (see English, 2005). Among individuals interviewed for this study, this was viewed as a particular problem for exploratory collection—efforts to detect or provide some warning of as yet-unknown terrorist activity—rather than the more investigative intelligence efforts involved in following leads gained from other information sources. One example is

---

12 According to a DOJ OIG report (2005b, p. iii):

> We found that the information collection efforts at the USAOs [U.S. Attorney General's office] differ markedly from district to district. The intelligence research specialists collect information through a variety of methods, such as reviewing case files, meeting with ATAC [Anti-Terrorism Advisory Council] members, and sharing information with their counterparts in other agencies. However, there was no uniformity in the sources used or in the types of information collected. Also, beyond basic requirements, EOUSA [Executive Office for United States Attorneys] has not identified the standard technology-based tools needed by intelligence research specialists to collect and analyze information.

13 DHS, Office of the Inspector General (2007b, p. 2). This observation was part of what led to the creation of the Office of Intelligence and Analysis to coordinate the activities.

14 See, for example, discussion in Posner (2006) or in WMD Commission (2005, pp. 468–471).

suspicious activity reports (SARs). In the financial arena, where transmitting SARs has long been an established part of efforts to counter criminal activity, there were concerns even before September 11 that the "volume of these reports was interfering with effective law enforcement" (Schulhofer, 2002, p. 52). Since September 11, the range of organizations obliged to submit such reports has broadened, and there have been calls from the private sector for better guidelines on what constitutes suspicious activity (Business Executives for National Security, 2003). Suspicious activity reporting through law enforcement and other channels into federal government organizations has been reported often to be of even less practical utility.[15] An NCTC official was quoted in the press observing, "In many instances the threshold for reporting is low, which makes it extremely difficult to evaluate some of this information" (Pincus, 2006. p. A5). There are reportedly many databases of different kinds of suspicious-activity reports across the government, and the value of the unverified information they contain has been called into question.[16]

To summarize, there are three major concerns with collection activities (1) cultural bias against exploratory collection and retaining data, (2) lack of coordination in domestic collection efforts, and (3) volume of data of questionable or poorly specified quality.

Analysis

A different set of problems is seen to plague the analysis component: (1) a lack of trained analysts, (2) a law enforcement culture that discounts exploratory analysis, (3) competing and uncoordinated analysis that clogs the system, and (4) insufficient analytic techniques and data to identify the domestic threat. Starting from questions by the 9/11 Commission concerns about analytical capabilities in the FBI—for intelligence rather than law enforcement work—a major focus has been on whether human resources are sufficiently trained to perform analytical functions. Subsequent inquiries, including that by the WMD Com-

---

15 Researcher discussions with federal officials.

16 Such practices also raise acceptability concerns about what information makes it into systems about American citizens that are discussed below.

mission, questioned how the FBI and other federal organizations are building their analytical capabilities, whether individuals in those roles are qualified for them, and, if so, whether they are actually being used for intelligence analysis. A 2007 follow-up report indicated that those defects had been largely overcome in the FBI (DOJ OIG, 2007b).[17]

Concerns were raised about the analytical capabilities at the state and local level as well: "State, local, tribal, and private sector entities lack a standard training program for homeland security intelligence analysts. This lack of standard training creates disparities in analyst capabilities, terminology, and approach to homeland security analysis" (DHS, Lessons Learned Information Sharing System, 2005, p. 4). Similar needs for standardized training and capability were echoed in an assessment of DOJ's multi-agency terrorism task forces (DOJ OIG, 2005a, p. ii).

Questions have been raised about bureaucratic competition in analysis among the key agencies. The WMD Commission report, for example, discussed at some length the effect of conflicting and duplicative analysis and warning (WMD Commission, 2005, pp. 288–295). Competing analyses can be insightful, and, in any case, different analytic operations in the Intelligence Community serve the different needs of consumers—from diplomacy and military operations, to policing. However, duplication can occur, as stated in the WMD Commission report (2005, p. 294):

> One incident in which a single raw intelligence report spurred five different agencies to write five separate pieces, all reaching the same conclusion. Not only were analysts' efforts redundant, but policymakers were then required to read through all five papers to look for subtle differences in perspective that could have been better conveyed in a single, coordinated paper.

At the federal level, individuals we spoke with during this study captured many of these concerns by posing the seemingly simple question—"Where is the center of analytical capability for domestic coun-

[17] See discussion in WMD Commission (2005, pp. 454–455) and DOJ OIG (2005a, 2005b).

terterrorism intelligence efforts supposed to be in the federal government?" NCTC is the central node for terrorism analysis at the federal level, but the main customer for its analytical efforts was characterized as "up"—the President—rather than "down"—the rest of the organizations involved in homeland security.

There was also an important question raised about the scale of terrorism that federal level domestic intelligence efforts are—or should be—designed to detect and prevent. Should efforts be focused on just large-scale attacks or should domestic intelligence efforts be focused on all terrorism in the United States? Should the focus be just on preventing another September 11–scale event or terrorism down to the level of groups such as the Earth Liberation Front? What about larger-scale attacks that fall between those two, such as the bombing of the Murrah Federal Building in Oklahoma City?

Both in the literature and among practitioners, another area of concern is the analytical capabilities to identify unknown clandestine terrorist cells planning operations inside the United States. The difficulty associated with detecting unobserved terrorist plots has been a driver of interest in data mining and automated analytical techniques using commercially available and other datasets.[18] Data mining is used in a variety of government efforts, and has been controversial, as discussed in more detail below.

Is data mining effective, given the limits in the techniques themselves and in the datasets available?[19] For example, the Markle Foundation Task Force reports that error rates in the commercial databases that are viewed as core inputs to such techniques are, at minimum, 1 to 2 percent (Markle Foundation Task Force, 2003, p. 60). This raises concerns about the implications of the false positive results—the flagging of innocent people as potential terrorists—of such techniques for

[18] See, for example, discussion in Seifert (2007) and U.S. General Accounting Office (2004).

[19] See, for example, Jonas and Harper (2006), Dempsey and Flint (2004, p. 1461), Harris (2006b), DeRosa (2004), and Technology and Privacy Advisory Council, U.S. Department of Defense, (2004).

both the people involved and the investigative organizations tasked with following up on the leads.

To summarize, four overarching concerns with domestic intelligence analysis are (1) a lack of appropriately skilled and trained staff, (2) a law enforcement culture that discounts exploratory analysis, (3) competing and uncoordinated analysis that clogs the system, and (4) insufficient analytic techniques and data to effectively identify as-yet-unknown domestic threats.

Information Sharing

In the reviews of intelligence efforts before the September 11 attacks, failures in information sharing both within and among federal agencies were cited as the central problem that needed to be fixed to prevent future attacks.[20] Much of the blame for information-sharing problems was placed on the "wall" that had been built between intelligence and law enforcement activities (9/11 Commission, 2004b). However, problems also included the fear that information that was recorded and shared would be discoverable in court proceedings—or become inadmissible in such proceedings (9/11 Commission, 2004a, p. 3); rivalries within agencies or among them for credit for counterterrorism successes; shortcomings in coordination efforts for the sharing of information (DHS, Office of the Inspector General, 2007b, p. 2); or even practical information and communication technology limitations that made it difficult to move information from one place to another or capture it in a usable form (9/11 Commission, 2004a, p. 3).

Though subsequent reviews, including that of the WMD Commission, have cited considerable improvement—notably due to the activities of the NCTC—concerns still exist about whether the "great deal of energy" being spent by Intelligence Community organizations on improving information sharing will actually yield "enduring insti-

---

[20] Some have questioned this assessment, characterizing the failures of information sharing that occurred before the attacks as anomalies against the backdrop of significant information flows among agencies: "The greatest perceptual problem about intelligence is the tendency to focus narrowly on whatever errors were committed relevant to the most recent case and to draw larger conclusions about overall performance without placing those data points in any larger context" (Pillar, 2004, p. 124).

tutional change required to address our current threat environment" (WMD Commission, 2005, pp. 286, 288). The commission specifically questioned whether transferring information by sharing personnel among agencies or in multi-agency centers (a broadly used approach in many information-sharing initiatives) is enough to provide all agencies' analysts sufficient access to other organizations' intelligence information for effective analysis (WMD Commission, 2005, p. 287).[21] These concerns were echoed in project interviews.

A series of questions have been raised since September 11 regarding the effectiveness of information-sharing efforts among different levels of government—between the federal government and homeland security and counterterrorism organizations at the state and local level. Even before September 11, some information-sharing mechanisms were in place, notably the FBI's JTTFs. Since the attacks, these mechanisms have expanded, and others, such as DHS's fusion centers, have been put in place. Assessments of the effectiveness of these and other information-sharing mechanisms differ, however. For example, one assessment of the task forces run by the Department of Justice concluded that "the state and local law enforcement agencies with members on a JTTF or ATAC [the Anti-Terrorism Advisory Council] were satisfied with the amount and type of terrorism information shared. In contrast, those law enforcement agencies that were outside of the metropolitan areas and that did not have task force or council members were not as satisfied" (DOJ OIG, 2005a, p. v). Interviewees suggested that substantial progress had been made regarding information sharing since September 11, though with plenty of room for improvement.

On the other hand, an assessment of the operation of fusion centers reached a more negative conclusion:

> Numerous fusion centers officials claim that although their center receives a substantial amount of information from federal agencies, they never seem to get the 'right information' or receive it in an efficient manner. According to many state fusion center

---

[21] Expressions of concern that information sharing has gone too far—given the security risks associated with sharing secrets with too many people—can also be found in the literature. See, for example, DOJ OIG (2003, p. 17).

> leaders, often-pertinent threat intelligence must be requested by fusion centers, rather than federal agencies being proactive in providing it. The obvious difficulty arises regarding the inability to request relevant threat information that is unknown to members of the fusion center. (Masse, 2006, p. 28)[22]

Other assessments have suggested a reluctance by federal agencies to share information and clashes of cultures between agencies at different levels of government (Wagner, 2007).

In response, federal officials have suggested that state and local officials assume more intelligence information is available than is actually the case.[23] Since September 11, the lack of federal security clearance for state and local officials was frequently raised as a barrier, limiting the ability to share raw intelligence or specific information about individual terrorist threats outside the federal government (DOJ OIG, 2003, p. 15).[24] Some sources report that substantial progress has been made in that area (Masse, 2006, p. 26). However, interviewees and members of the project expert panel still highlighted over-classification and lack of cleared staff in all relevant organizations as a barrier to information sharing.

While assessments differ on just how information is flowing to states and localities from the federal government, most agree that

---

22 Some actions are already in process to address some of the concerns at the time of this writing (Larence, 2007).

23 For example, see discussion in DOJ OIG (2003, p. 16).

24 It is difficult to determine with certainty, and report in an unclassified document, specifically what types of information cannot be shared because of clearance concerns and what the implications of it not being shareable for the activities of organizations involved in terrorism prevention missions at other levels of government. Based on the types of information mentioned or specifically redacted in unclassified public documents, it is clear that it includes raw intelligence and specific information on the types of threats identified against U.S. homeland targets (see, for example, DOJ OIG, 2003, p. 53). Examples cited in other contexts have included specific vulnerability information produced by federal agencies being classified for infrastructure facilities (See U.S. Government Accountability Office, 2005).

Another challenge in sharing is originator control (or ORCON) requirements, under which individual federal agencies keep control of how information they produce is shared, limiting the ability to disseminate it through other agencies' information sharing channels (e.g., JTTFs or fusion centers).

the system in place does not yet represent a truly two-directional information-sharing effort to allow useful information to flow back to the federal government.[25] There are also significant concerns about duplication in the system creating problems for state and local intelligence efforts.[26,27] The WMD Commission in particular cited the many

> redundant lines of communication through which terrorism-related information is passed—for example, through the Joint Terrorism Task Forces, Anti-Terrorism Advisory Councils, Homeland Security Information Network, TTIC Online, Law Enforcement Online Network, Centers for Disease Control alerts, and Public Health Advisories, to name just a few—present a deluge of information for which state, local, and tribal authorities are neither equipped nor trained to process, prioritize, and disseminate. (WMD Commission, 2005, p. 287).

Others have echoed this concern about duplicative information technology systems in the domestic intelligence enterprise (U.S. Government Accountability Office, 2007; Masse, O'Neil, and Rollins, 2007, p. 30). While sharing relevant, timely, and actionable information is certainly valuable for counterterrorism efforts, "indiscriminate reporting of unverified information, without regard to information quality, reliability or usefulness, or without considering the receiving agency's ability to analyze the information, is not the effective information sharing environment" that is needed to contribute to better protecting the country from the threat of terrorism (Markle Foundation Task Force, 2006, p. 19).

---

25 DHS, Lessons Learned Information Sharing System (2005); Clarke and Beers (2006).

26 It should be noted that not all instances of apparent duplication have been faulted. A DOJ Inspector general review of DOJ's counterterrorism task forces found that, although there were multiple groups with apparently similar remits, that there was not "significant duplication of effort" and that they were "distinct yet complementary forums for sharing terrorism-related information and intelligence and investigating terrorist threats." (DOJ OIG, 2005a, p. ii.)

27 This belief was echoed by individuals interviewed for the project.

With respect to actually *acting* against identified terrorist suspects, relatively few questions have been raised about the effectiveness of the current domestic intelligence enterprise. Indeed, in the post–September 11 environment, the unwillingness to risk any suspected terrorist plot coming to fruition led to criticism of the FBI for acting "too quickly" against identified plots and settling for filing charges other than terrorism.[28] Doing so was viewed as sacrificing potential intelligence-gathering opportunities where identified individuals might identify other yet unknown conspirators. The Bureau has reportedly changed its approach in recent years.[29] Similarly, barring breakdowns in information sharing, there have also been few questions raised about the ability of law enforcement organizations at other levels of government to act effectively against suspects—in considering the effectiveness of domestic counterterrorism intelligence, most concerns focus on the development, analysis, and sharing of the information needed to act, not the ability to do so.

To summarize, two overarching concerns with domestic intelligence action are (1) continuing concern about information sharing across the intelligence–law enforcement seam; and (2) the effectiveness of information sharing across different levels of government.

Implications for Privacy and Civil Liberties

As noted earlier, actions by domestic intelligence and law enforcement organizations in pursuit of counterterrorism objectives may affect individual privacy and civil liberties, or at least appear to infringe on them.[30] Given the history of domestic intelligence activities in the

[28] This issue bridges on concerns about effectiveness and acceptability, discussed in the next section, and the belief that the filing of less serious charges undermines the legitimacy of the expanded powers provided for counterterrorism intelligence. See, for example, remarks of David Cole reported at "Do We Need an MI5?" (2003).

[29] See discussion of both the original policy and the more recent shifts in Block (2007).

[30] Interestingly, among interviewees for this study—the majority of whom were individuals within organizations in the domestic intelligence enterprise—views were split over whether there would be cause for concern regarding civil liberties if a new agency was created.

United States, the potential effects of domestic intelligence activities on individual privacy, civil rights and civil liberties, and, consequently, the nature of American democracy are always central in policy debate on these issues. The perceptions of the panel of experts we consulted for this study varied considerably in their judgments about the current system but skewed toward concern that it is only moderately effective at safeguarding privacy and civil liberties, with effective oversight appearing to be a shortfall.

Views of what privacy entails differ, ranging from the idea that individuals or organizations should be able to converse or act in complete privacy, to much more limited definitions. From most viewpoints, privacy is inherently reduced by the collection and storage of information—whether those activities are carried out by the government or by other organizations or individuals. Thus, there are inescapable privacy concerns associated with many types of intelligence activity. Intelligence efforts can be designed in ways that are more or less intrusive, but there will always be some tradeoffs to be made. Weighing the potential harms caused by reductions in privacy against the potential gains in security caused by government having access to more information is an inherently political exercise. As a result, no analysis can provide a "right" answer as to what balances should be struck and what costs are entailed in doing so.

One prominent concern is the changes in regulation and practices that have enabled the government to gather information, or access directly information gathered by others, about an increasing number of Americans. Here, a much-debated example is the USA PATRIOT Act's expansion of the ways that agencies could use internally generated national security letters to request information. Collecting information on American citizens without judicial warrants was also the central part of the controversy surrounding the so-called Terrorist Surveillance Program, under which the NSA intercepted communications on both foreign nationals and American citizens.[31] Other areas of concern have

---

[31] Ongoing litigation alleges additional domestic interception activities of Internet communications traffic, and that these activities have not been acknowledged. See, for example, Lichtblau and Risen (2005), Eggen (2007), and Poe (2006).

been the use of private-sector databases and the use of data mining of large datasets of personal information,[32] accumulating data on individuals that have nothing to do with terrorism in government databases,[33] and the risks to individuals of government storage and sharing of personal information.[34]

While privacy is the preeminent civil liberty at issue, intelligence activities can also bear on other liberties—for example, if the result of intelligence collection and use is the detention or arrest of innocent people or discrimination against particular individuals or groups. Other effects may be less visible but still of concern. For example, civil liberties organizations and analysts have raised concern about a "chilling effect" from communications monitoring or information collection on individuals' willingness to exercise their freedom of expression, dissent, or assembly.[35]

Questions have been raised about the effect of counterterrorism measures on particular ethnic or other groups,[36] the potential for inaccurate data to lead to action against innocent individuals,[37] and con-

---

[32] DHS, Data Privacy and Integrity Advisory Committee (2006); Seifert (2007); Dempsey and Flint (2004); Birrer (2005); "Feds Sharpen Secret Tools for Data Mining" (2006); Technology and Privacy Advisory Council, U.S. Department of Defense (2004); and Shane Harris (2006a).

[33] American Civil Liberties Union (2007).

[34] Technology and Privacy Advisory Council, U.S. Department of Defense (2004, pp. 36–42).

[35] "Not only can direct awareness of surveillance make a person feel extremely uncomfortable, but it can also cause that person to alter her behavior. Surveillance can lead to self-censorship and inhibition . . . there can be an even greater chilling effect when people are generally aware of the possibility of surveillance, but are never sure if they are being watched at any particular moment" (Solove, 2006, pp. 493–495). See also discussion in Taipale (Winter 2004–2005). The impact of a chilling effect has also been invoked with respect to members of intelligence organizations—to describe the effect on intelligence practices after the reforms of the 1970s were imposed (Wildhorn, Jenkins and Lavin, 1982, pp. 100–101).

[36] This has been characterized by some as a not unexpected tendency given the difficulty of identifying terrorists in the general population—driving action by the data that are most straightforward to collect, rather than focusing on collecting the data that is most important. See discussion in Martin (2004, p. 11). See also WMD Commission (2005, p. 456).

[37] DeRosa (2004, pp. 13–14), Chesney (2003), DOJ OIG (2006), and Davis (2003).

cerns about government agencies and individuals within them adhering to established policies and rules for the collection and use of information on American citizens.[38,39]

The exploratory nature of domestic intelligence is probably the most problematic from the perspective of public acceptance. That is so because it is difficult to establish boundaries: Witness the COINTELPRO operations in which the expression of dissent by individuals and organizations was deemed enough to make them targets of intelligence activities. Recent instances in which the activities of antiwar groups have been recorded in intelligence databases or monitored by undercover law enforcement operations have raised similar concerns.[40] If protest or dissent may result in surveillance or even more significant action by government, individuals or groups may be fearful of acting. If attendance at religious gatherings leads to—or is thought to lead to—surveillance, individuals may be less likely to go.[41] As a result, the perceived privacy and liberties effects of current programs can drive elements of public debate on intelligence.[42]

The next section of this report discusses different approaches to the range of problems identified with regard to domestic intelligence.

---

[38] For example, Solomon (2007), DOJ OIG (2007a), DHS, Office of the Inspector General (2007a), Technology and Privacy Advisory Council, U.S. Department of Defense (2004, p. 3); DHS, Office of the Inspector General (2005), Nakashima (2007), Koontz (2007), Fay (1998), and Technology and Privacy Advisory Council, U.S. Department of Defense (2004, p. 40).

[39] Members of the expert panel were critical of oversight in the current system, some even dismissing it completely, and flagged it as an important target for Congressional attention, whatever decision was made about the creation of a new domestic intelligence agency.

[40] For example, American Civil Liberties Union (2007).

[41] See, for example, reported discussions with mosque attendees in Moss and Nordberg (2003).

[42] An example of this dynamic is clear in the comments of CIA Director Michael Hayden after the 2007 release of the documents known as the "family jewels" detailing some of the agency's past misdeeds: At its release, he was quoted as saying that "when the government withholds information, myth and misinformation often 'fill the vacuum like a gas'" (Shane, 2007), driving shifts in the public's view of the legitimacy and acceptability of intelligence efforts.

CHAPTER FOUR

A Range of Options for Improving Domestic Intelligence

The concerns about domestic intelligence described in the previous chapter have to do with *how* organizations work, not the outcomes of that work. This is because it is difficult to specify, and even harder to measure, the relationship between domestic intelligence activities and counterterrorism success. Does the fact that we have had no domestic terrorist attacks since September 11 mean that U.S. domestic intelligence and other efforts to counter terrorism are good enough, that we were simply lucky, that the threat has been overestimated, or some combination of these explanations?

In the absence of detailed assessments of particular agencies and their performance, which explicitly was not our charter, we use the concerns identified in the last chapter to explore whether reorganization or other approaches might improve domestic intelligence arrangements, to the extent those concerns remain valid today. The concerns cluster in three areas:

- There is lingering concern that domestic intelligence is overshadowed by the law enforcement culture, which constrains the use and further improvement of these capabilities.
- Many people suggest that collaboration across the seams of organizations and levels of government involved in domestic intelligence is inconsistent, yet collaboration is critical to successful counterterrorism operations.

- Some believe that management of information related to counterterrorism efforts is inefficient, constraining the ability of organizations to collect, share, protect, and utilize information effectively.

Running across these themes are concerns about the effects that changes in counterterrorism domestic intelligence will have on privacy and civil liberties. The next sections describe the range of approaches that could potentially contribute to addressing these concerns and examine their relevance to each cluster of problems.

Potential Approaches

Almost all post-mortems of major crises, including September 11, produce clarion calls for more money and high-level attention to the shortfalls believed to have resulted in the crisis. The fight against terrorism has surely received both. More specifically, though, against the definitions of the problem, what are possible approaches? Certainly, changing the structure of the enterprise—because domestic intelligence exists through the efforts of many organizations—is one approach, but it is only one. A longer list might start there, and this list surely could be extended.

- *Restructure the enterprise:* Reorganization is a frequent response to crisis, for it demonstrates that action is being taken. Though structure has a range of effects on the activities of the organization and its members, formal structures and linkages are not the only determiners of behavior. In general, there is no perfect organization, for any enterprise will leave seams that need to be bridged. The risk associated with reorganization, one explored in more detail in Chapter Five, is that doing so will disrupt productive relationships that are already in place, especially those between federal law enforcement organizations and state and local officials, requiring officials and individual members of the organization to scramble to adjust.

- *Increase resources:* In the simplest case, providing more money or resources (people, technology, information) can be a response to perceived shortfalls. Usually, this approach presumes that the organization is doing appropriate tasks, just not enough of them. In other cases, additional resources can be an incentive for organizations—either at the federal level or elsewhere in the system—to change their behavior, doing more of some specific task or taking on some new mission.
- *Improve management systems:* It is hard not to favor improving management, but the challenge is how to do it. There is a focus on improving management in governance, exemplified by the Government Performance and Results Act of 1993 (P. L. 103-62) and its focus on developing ways to measure the outcome of government activities. Since most government agencies lack anything close to business's "bottom line," the need is to define outcome metrics against which to judge the outputs of government action. As stressed several times in this report, that is a special challenge for intelligence, all the more so for strategic intelligence. More-tangible examples of efforts to improve management include institutionalized internal audit and oversight functions to monitor behavior and correct problems.[1] Such activities could include formalized internal independent oversight activities (e.g., inspectors general) or routine oversight as part of day-to-day functions.
- *Improve use of technology:* This approach amounts to changing the production function for government agencies. This is fairly straightforward for agencies whose activities focus on stable processes (e.g., the Social Security Administration). In such cases, improving technology can improve databases, identification of recipients, ways of transferring money, and the like. For domestic intelligence, exploratory collection in particular requires the use of technology to manage databases, detect patterns, retain dis-

---

[1] For example, systems to identify and punish unauthorized access to files or other information by government employees. A good example of such processes are the management mechanisms in place to address the problem of Internal Revenue Service employees accessing taxpayers records (Herman, 2007).

carded hypotheses, and perform other information-management tasks.[2]

- *Enhance collaboration:* To increase collaboration among separate organizations, the two most frequent techniques are to create coordinating bodies or processes or to designate a lead agency. To be effective, collaboration mechanisms must overcome the separate interests of the organizations the effort is seeking to bridge, either by producing common incentives for cooperative behavior or linking the success of the participating organizations tightly to the cooperative action. Without incentives for collaboration and cooperation, as well as clear guidance as to the regulations governing group behavior, the separate interests of the participating organizations will threaten the effectiveness of the effort.
- *Change laws:* For agencies whose actions are constrained (or required) by law, the laws can be changed. The USA PATRIOT Act, for example, loosened the legal standards for FISA surveillance, thus making it easier to follow suspected terrorists. Other shifts in laws could prohibit activities of concern.[3]
- *Change regulations or orders:* Regulations and operating procedures within organizations shape activity, and problems in performance can be addressed by altering them. The "wall" separating law enforcement and intelligence before September 11 was partly statutory but also partly administrative, and could be affected by simple administrative changes. After September 11, for instance, the FBI merged what had been separate case categories for intelligence and enforcement directed at terrorism. The federal government can use regulations to affect not only its own behavior but also that of other levels of law enforcement as well as private citizens. Funding for states and localities almost always come with regulations attached.

---

[2] A number of observers have noted that pre–September 11 intelligence made little use of formal methods or machines. See Johnston (2005) and Treverton and Gabbard (2008).

[3] For example, interviewees indicated that confusion about roles and responsibilities among agencies in the domestic intelligence enterprise could be addressed through legislative action that falls well short of major reorganization.

- *Improve leadership:* Calls for better leadership after crises are frequent. The most obvious way to try to improve leadership is to simply change the leaders as, for example, the Federal Emergency Management Agency (FEMA) did in reaction to public anger over its handling of Hurricane Katrina rescue and recovery operations in 2005. However, actually improving leadership across an organization is harder and requires time and attention to recruitment, incentives, and mid-career training. One element of leadership is effective oversight of organizational activities to ensure that leaders are both aware of and responsible for the actions of the organization.
- *Improve policy:* Sometimes the right response is not to change how government organizations act but, rather, the policy they seek to implement. If organizations have been tasked with attempting to achieve the wrong policy goals, problems achieving positive outcomes should not surprise.
- *Change the culture:* Organizational cultures develop around missions and resist change. Changing culture requires drive from the top accompanied by changes in incentives and training that cause individual members to change their behavior in sufficient numbers to alter the way the entire organization performs its tasks. At times, the ability to retire large cohorts of personnel or acquire large numbers of new recruits can help, though the transition in staff can also bring gaps in capability. The transformation of the FBI is just such an effort at changing culture, driven from the top and guided by a 100-person Strategic Execution Team (SET) representing 27 field offices.[4]

---

[4] The creation in 2007 of the SET was explicitly intended to push the pace of transforming the FBI into an intelligence-led organization. Its focus has been standardizing field intelligence practices, streamlining intelligence production and dissemination, and enhancing the FBI's human source development capabilities. As of October 2008, the initial rollout of organizational changes, along with new training in field office roles and responsibilities, had been completed in 32 of 56 field offices. Three-quarters of agents and intelligence analysts had completed the training in such core intelligence functions as domain awareness, tactical collection, and production.

Arraying Approaches Against Domestic Intelligence Concerns

The question motivating this study is an organizational one—the feasibility of reorganizing domestic intelligence efforts by creating a new counterterrorism intelligence agency—but that is only one possible approach to addressing perceived concerns. To map the broader context of the assessment, it is worth examining how the other possible solutions array against the concerns that have been identified. Table 4.1 summarizes that mapping.

If the FBI is dominated by a law enforcement and case-based approach: If this were the concern, including that both collection and analysis are dominated by operational support to law enforcement, then creating a new intelligence organization could indeed be one logical approach to addressing the problem. It is the focus of the next chapter. But, as Table 4.1 suggests, a number of other solutions could also be relevant. Increasing resources might be necessary but not sufficient, since organizations tend to respond to more money by doing more of what they were already doing. In any event, the FBI's budget more than doubled between 2001 and 2008, from $3.1 billion to $6.4 billion.

Less dramatic organizational change could also be relevant. Indeed, the Bureau created the National Security Branch to emphasize prevention and intelligence, particularly in the counterterrorism mission. That was part of an effort to change culture in a number of ways, from recentralizing the management of terrorism cases, to training, to rapid growth, which meant that more than half of FBI agents now have served for less than five years and so have not known an organization dominated by pure law enforcement. Changed laws, such as the USA PATRIOT Act, made it easier to collect counterterrorism intelligence, especially of the more exploratory sort, and changed regulations had the same effect, plus they dismantled the wall between intelligence and law enforcement.

Finally, leadership can be critical. In the FBI's case, Robert Mueller had been on the job one week before September 11, and he quickly determined to change the FBI's mission and made a strong case for doing so both inside the organization and with outsiders and authoriz-

Table 4.1
Expressed Concerns and Possible Responses

Expressed Concern	Possible Responses
If the FBI is dominated by a law enforcement and case-based approach; and if, as a result, collection is dominated by case requirements and analysis is dominated by operational support . . .	. . . then increase resources, change organization, change culture, change laws, change regulations or orders, and/or improve leadership.
If the FBI, CIA, and other agencies do not talk to each other . . .	. . . then change organization, change culture, change laws, change regulations or orders, enhance collaboration, and/or improve leadership.
If too much poor-quality information is collected, and collection efforts are too uncoordinated . . .	. . . then change regulations or orders, enhance collaboration, and/or improve leadership.
If analysis is fragmented and sometimes conflicting; and if the National Counterterrorism Center, which acts as a central clearinghouse, mostly provides information to the President rather than to other intelligence organizations . . .	. . . then change organization, change regulations or orders, enhance collaboration, and/or improve leadership.
If it is difficult to move information and analysis across the domestic intelligence enterprise . . .	. . . then increase resources, change regulations or orders, enhance collaboration, and/or improve leadership.

ers, from the administration to Congress. Opinions will differ on how effective the internal changes in the Bureau have been, and only time will tell. But the reshaping that Mueller is driving illustrates many of the approaches relevant to addressing the role of the culture and mission of the Bureau in the domestic intelligence problem.

If the FBI, CIA, and other agencies do not talk to each other: The September 11 attacks provided graphic testimony to the need for improved interagency communication. A major change in organization, such as the creation of a separate domestic intelligence service, could improve communication, for such a service might find it easier to work with fellow intelligence services. Lesser organizational change, such as the creation of the National Security Branch as an in-house intelligence agency, could also be relevant. Changing the culture of interagency cooperation was surely facilitated, in all agencies, by the shock of September 11, but could also be advanced by training, more joint assignments, and other personnel approaches. For instance, now analysts from the FBI, CIA, and other agencies sit side-by-side at NCTC and in each other's headquarters

Changing laws could be relevant, and changing regulations or orders surely would be. For instance, before September 11 the FBI was required to provide information to the Director of Central Intelligence (DCI) only if that information was "essential to the national security" and only "upon the written request" of the DCI.[5] The FBI also was responsible for protecting material before federal grand juries, and although sharing with the CIA and intelligence agencies was possible, in practice information was shared only with a court order. The force of internal rules was all too evident in the misadventures between the two agencies over the two September 11 hijackers, Khalid al-Mihdhar and Nawaf al-Hazmi, and those rules could be changed.

Several efforts have been made to enhance interagency collaboration. One was the creation of the NCTC, with the idea that it would be not only a central coordinator of terrorism intelligence but also a kind of counterterrorism "campus," with large chunks of both the CIA's Counterterrorism Center and the FBI's Counterterrorism Division colocated there, along with smaller counterterrorism contingents from other agencies. The expansion of the JTTFs has provided one among a number of possible locales for joint assignments of CIA and FBI officers and all levels of government as well as other government agencies. The creation of the DNI has provided for more collaboration mostly at the strategic level, but it also added another facilitator of and incentive for day-to-day cooperation. And leadership in both agencies committed to working together has been critical.

If too much poor-quality information is collected, and collection efforts are uncoordinated: A variety of approaches could be adopted to address perceived problems in collection and coordination of collection activities. A clear requirements process could lay out a common map of the types of information needed and provide a way to coordinate col-

---

5 National Security Act of 1947, 50 U.S.C. 403, Sec. 102 (e).

lection across the sprawling domestic intelligence enterprise.[6] Improved databases and information technology could make it easier for different elements of the domestic intelligence enterprise to "know what it already knows"[7] and limit duplicative collection.[8]

Thus far, most changes in regulations or orders have been intended to produce *more* collection, but changes would be relevant in the other direction as well. Raising the threshold for suspicious-activity reporting might be one example: Even though there were concerns before September 11 that the volume and low quality of such reporting was getting in the way of effective law enforcement, changes since have increased rather than decreased suspicious-activity reporting (Schulhofer, 2002, p. 52; Business Executives for National Security, 2003).

Enhancing collaboration, including the tasks of prioritizing federal collection efforts and integrating local and federal law enforcement, might take several forms, none of which appear especially promising. Enhanced collaboration is the goal of DNI's National Intelligence Coordination Center (NIC-C), but that center is new and its reach into domestic collection is uncertain. The FBI or some other agency might be designated the lead agency for domestic collection, much as the CIA's Deputy Director for Operations is the National HUMINT (Human Intelligence) Manager. As always, leadership will be critical.

Organizational change doesn't seem very relevant on the collection side. Even if a new domestic agency were designated the lead agency for domestic collection, it would also be yet one more collector, and the efforts of the embedded federal collectors and of state and local authorities would continue. Rather, the best solutions might be process-oriented—for example, creating better mechanisms to ensure two-way information flow and feedback to organizations that provide

---

6 State and local organizations have criticized the lack of a consolidated requirements process for homeland security intelligence to ensure that collection matches the needs of homeland security organizations (DHS, Lessons Learned Information Sharing System, 2005, p. 4).

7 See, for example, discussion of knowledge management for intelligence in Lahneman (2004).

8 DHS, Office of the Inspector General, (2007b, p. 2). This observation was part of what led to the creation of the Office of Intelligence and Analysis to coordinate the activities.

intelligence information. Or perhaps better incentives to collect higher-quality data could be implemented—for example, the federal intelligence enterprise could link financial support to state and local organizations to the intelligence information they provide (this would almost be a "fee for service" model).

If analysis is fragmented and sometimes conflicting; if NCTC acts as a central clearinghouse, but it mostly provides information to the President rather than to other intelligence organizations: Centralizing analysis in a new organization might be conceivable if that organization somehow both absorbed NCTC's role as an analytic clearinghouse for the executive branch (upward) and added to it the task of sharing with state and local agencies (downward). Colocation of analytical efforts could reduce fragmentation and the potential for conflicts but could do so at the price of productive variety and alternative analysis. Regulations or even laws might be changed to give NCTC even more authority to coordinate terrorism intelligence and to task it with providing material to be shared downward. Under current law, DHS has the mandate for assembling counterterrorism intelligence, but in fact NCTC has taken that role.

NCTC is also probably the main candidate to be strengthened in an effort to enhance collaboration, but the DNI and the Deputy DNI for Analysis could also play roles. The Deputy DNI for Analysis chairs the National Intelligence Council (NIC), which produces National Intelligence Estimates and serves as a kind of honest broker among the analytic arms of the intelligence agencies. However, given the NIC's origins in the CIA—it now works for the DNI—it has conceived its mandate as *foreign* intelligence, and domestic intelligence remains something of a stepchild in both the NIC and the larger DNI operation.[9]

If it is difficult to move information and analysis across the domestic intelligence enterprise: Notice that while the other concerns about U.S. domestic intelligence enterprise locate the issue at the federal level, this broadens the concern to the entire domestic intelligence enterprise,

[9] The National Intelligence Estimate entitled *The Terrorist Threat to the U.S. Homeland* (National Intelligence Council, 2007) is a recent exception.

which includes organizations at all levels of government and some in the private sector. This implies that the federal government will have fewer, and sometimes only indirect, levers—such as the conditions placed on grant funding or standard setting—for affecting the behavior of state and local authorities, private-sector firms, and individual citizens. For that reason, this definition is worth considering in somewhat greater detail than the other definitions.

"Information sharing" is the current mantra in Washington, and a number of initiatives across the range of options are already underway to address this concern. Efforts aimed at enhancing collaboration to address information sharing include the JTTFs and the DHS fusion centers, which have even been argued to amount to a *de facto* "decentralized domestic intelligence agency."[10] DHS supports the fusion centers with both money and intelligence analysts. Funding connected with these programs represent a resource-based approach to addressing this problem.

Technological solutions are similarly suggested as approaches to this concern, an approach reflected in the reports of the Markle Foundation Task Force, which proposed meeting domestic intelligence needs through creation of a "trusted information network for homeland security" (2003) to "empower local efforts, nationally coordinated" (2002, p. 2). Similar goals and approaches are echoed in the Information Sharing Environment (ISE) program in the Office of the Director of National Intelligence, which is seeking to build a "future ISE that represents a trusted partnership among all levels of government in the United States, the private sector, and our foreign partners" (Program Manager, Information Sharing Environment, 2006, p. xiii). A variety of technological systems, including the Homeland Security Information Network (HSIN) and other law enforcement systems are also technology-based approaches to this problem.[11]

---

10 See, for example, characterization of the fusion center program by the American Civil Liberties Union quoted in Masse (2006, p. 11).

11 As discussed previously, views on the utility of these systems vary across organizations within the domestic intelligence enterprise. HSIN has been criticized regarding its usability and the information it contains and, near the completion of this study, a significant reworking of the system was announced (see Hsu and O'Harrow, 2008).

Beyond the variety of ongoing efforts, changes in regulations and orders and improvements in leadership could be applicable to addressing information-sharing weaknesses.

CHAPTER FIVE

Assessing Structural Options

Perhaps paradoxically, if the expert panel RAND assembled did not assess current arrangements very positively, neither were the experts enthusiastic about possible organizational alternatives. The four alternatives we offered were all assessed in the middle of a scale from "very good" to "very poor." The highest score went to the idea of an autonomous service within an existing agency (a more autonomous version of the FBI's existing National Security Branch), largely because the experts perceived the transition costs for it to be lower than for the other alternatives.

The paradox suggests that the experts were pessimistic about the ability of the U.S. government to do much better, were more sanguine about the threat than some political commentary would have it, or both. When asked how much the risk of terrorism has been reduced since September 11, the experts' response hinted at an explanation along the lines of "we're not doing well but are doing better and, besides, the near-term threat has been hyped." Notwithstanding their negative assessments of current capabilities, they still thought the risk of a major attack had diminished by a third.

This chapter and the next turn in detail to the specific organizational question: If a new organization were to be established to focus on domestic intelligence, how should it be designed in order to address the problems described in the previous chapter? We begin the chapter by outlining key points that emerged from the project's review of the experience of six other nations, five of which have a separate domestic service, and it draws some lessons for the United States from those cases. We then look at work on mission and function, organization and reorganization, and processes and information flows in both the public and private sectors. This approach can hardly provide definitive answers, but it can provide pointers to thinking about not just specific choices about a separate domestic intelligence organization but also about the domestic intelligence enterprise in general.

As lead-in to the next chapter's totting up of the pros and cons of creating a separate service, this chapter concludes with the two main forms a separate service might take. That is, if the goal of a new organization were better intelligence collection and analysis, along with a strengthened national domestic intelligence enterprise more generally, then how would different structures affect the ability to address this problem? As always in public policy, the devil is in the details, and so some of the very specific issues, such as where a separate service would be located and what specific authorities its mandate would include, would make a big difference—a point that also stands out in the review of previous government reorganizations.

Experiences of Other Democracies

In this age of terrorism, many countries face variations of the same challenges that confront the United States. One of those is based on the realization that because terrorists respect neither national borders nor organizational distinctions, nations need to collect more information on their inhabitants and strengthen connections between intelligence and law enforcement, trying to do both with as little cost to privacy and liberty as possible. In these circumstances, we examined Britain, Canada, Australia, Germany, France, and Sweden.[1] All are countries with democratic norms and governance similar to the United States, and the inclusion of Canada and Germany provides countries with federal structures more akin to those of the United States than those of

[1] This section draws on the cases produced by RAND colleagues, to whom we are grateful. Peter Chalk was responsible for Australia and Canada, Lindsay Clutterbuck for Britain, Richard Warnes for France and Germany, and Gregory Treverton for Sweden.

more unitary states such as Britain. Sweden, a smaller country, affords another kind of comparison, since it alone of the six has a domestic security service more akin to the U.S. FBI, responsible for both intelligence and policing.

We examined each nation schematically, across a range of attributes from history and mission, to leadership, management, organization and oversights. In the discussion that follows, we present the highlights most relevant to thinking about a separate service in the United States.

Creation and Key History

Domestic intelligence arrangements have usually been created and almost always shaped by the perceived need, during war or other national crisis, to keep tabs on possible enemies within the nation's borders. For instance, the Australian Security Intelligence Organization (ASIO) was created in 1949 following revelations that the Soviet Union was running a spy ring in the Australian Government. The Swedish Security Service (Säkershetspolisen, or SäPo) was created in 1914, dismantled after the war, then recreated in 1938, as war clouds again gathered.

The British service, MI-5, has the oldest roots, arguably running back to Elizabethan times when principal secretaries of the court ran spies at home and abroad to protect the Queen and her regime. The Metropolitan Police Force, founded in 1829, soon began deploying officers in plain clothes to gather political intelligence. In 1883 the Force's Special Branch came into being as a kind of intelligence service to deal with a campaign of bomb attacks being waged on the streets of Britain in the name of Irish republicanism. The Home Secretary set up a parallel "Secret Service" to assist the Branch, but the result was more infighting than crime fighting, and the new service was sharply curtailed, leaving the Special Branch to keep tabs on Irish and other potential enemies within.

It was the specter of war that led, in 1909, to the formation of a "Secret Service Bureau," referred to later as MI-5. The organization was established under military auspices, though with a retired head of Special Branch as deputy. With the outbreak of war in 1914, the service's staff mushroomed, from 14 in July 1914 to 844 by November 1918.

A second motivation in the shaping, and sometimes the creation of, domestic intelligence services has been the concern that previous arrangements had led, or might lead, to abuses of the liberties of the nation's inhabitants. The sharpest instance among these services is Canada, where a 1984 law transferred the domestic intelligence function from the Security Service of the Royal Canadian Mounted Police (SS-RCMP) to a new agency separate from policing, the Canadian Security Intelligence Service (CSIS), to provide both a more solid legal basis for and more rigorous oversight of domestic intelligence. [2]

Mission and Critical Capabilities

All of the services save Sweden's are specifically walled off from police or other "executive" power. The description of MI-5 in a 1963 British report is representative: "They have no executive powers [and] are a relatively small professional organization charged with the task of countering espionage, subversion and sabotage."[3] Given their creation in wartime, the original driving mission of all of the services was counterintelligence, and the age of terrorism has required several of them to reshape that mission. For instance, at CSIS's inception in 1984, the counterintelligence mission consumed perhaps as much as 80 percent of the Service's resources, and the numbers were similar for Australia and Sweden in that time period.

In contrast, Britain, Germany and France had devoted considerable attention to terrorism well before 2001—in Britain's case the focus has been primarily on the Irish Republican Army, and in Germany's it has been mostly on such home-grown organizations as the Baader-Meinhoff Gang, which developed into the *Rote Armee Fraktion* (Red Army Faction), but also on international terrorism, which developed from the early 1970s and was underscored by the "Black Septem-

---

[2] Interview by Peter Chalk, Washington D.C., May 2007. See also Canadian Society for Industrial Security (2005).

[3] Directive issues by Sir David Maxwell Fyffe, September 24, 1952, quoted in Denning (1992, p.91).

ber" kidnapping and murder of Israeli athletes at the Munich Olympic Games in 1972.[4] As early as 1993, Germany's *Bundesamt für Verfassungsschutz* (BfV), or Federal Office for the Protection of the Constitution, allocated 70 percent of its resources to counterterrorism, about half of it Irish-related. For MI-5, counterterrorism made up 80 percent of its work in 2007 (17 percent domestic, including Irish-related, 63 percent international), 5 percent was counterespionage, and 2 percent counterproliferation. For its part, France's *Direction de la Surveillance du Territoire* (DST) or Territorial Surveillance Directorate has been engaged against terrorism since the Algeria wars of the 1950s and now concentrates on the 5 million or more Algerian and North African Muslims in France, amidst growing radicalization of alienated youth in the *banlieue* (suburbs) of major French cities and Iraq, and CSIS has been given some foreign intelligence authorities.

Almost by definition as intelligence services, their main capabilities are covertly collecting and then analyzing information from domestic sources. CSIS is typical in the range of its activities—from covert observation, to running agents, to more intrusive special investigation techniques, such as electronic or video surveillance, bugging and wiretapping of private communications, intercepting and opening mail, installing tracking devices, taking DNA samples, and covert search-and entry operations. Especially for Australia, Canada, and Sweden, which have no foreign espionage service, the era of terrorism has carried the uncomfortable realization that their activities cannot be confined to home (European Commission for Democracy Through Law, 2007). This realization has been all the more pronounced for Canada's CSIS given its own forward role in support of U.S.-led military operations into Afghanistan and Iraq.

ASIO, CSIS, and BfV tend to rely more heavily than the others on open-source, or "gray," information. For the first two, much of that comes from local ethnic and other communities, mostly obtained from regular interviews with local leaders and representatives. Meetings are both "declared," when the ASIO affiliation is specifically acknowledged, and "undeclared," when it is not.

---

4 See Reeve (2005).

Leadership and Human Capital

All the services have grown rapidly since September 11, and are relatively large in comparison with the FBI, which has 12,000 agents and 30,000 employees in a much larger country. Like others, MI-5 doubled in size between 2001 (1,800 personnel) and 2008 (about 3,600 personnel), after having gently declined in size after the end of the Cold War (Brown, 2006). ASIO had a complement of 1,400 as of October 2007 and is set to expand to around 1,800 personnel by 2010, the bulk assigned to dedicated counterterrorism duties.[5] CSIS had 2,423 people as of 2007. The German BfV had some 2,500 in central offices in Cologne and Berlin in 2006, with about 2,900 in its 16 regional offices.[6] Interestingly, women are more heavily represented in most of the services than in other intelligence agencies, accounting, for instance, for more than half of MI-5.

Virtually all of the services draw their senior leadership from within the service. That is true of MI-5. For its part, France's DST has been considered the elite of the French *Police Nationale*, from whom the majority of its staff are seconded. Likewise, its leadership appears to be recruited predominantly among senior police officials. For several services, though, the senior-most job is an exception, with the director general or equivalent drawn from a neighboring profession or service. For ASIO, that has been primarily the diplomatic service; for Sweden, historically, it has been an outsider but someone with experience in police, prosecution, or the Justice Ministry.

Management and Process

Typically, the heads of the services report directly to the government's senior justice or interior official and through that official to a relevant cabinet committee, since all the countries have parliamentary governments rather than presidential systems like the United States. In Britain, the Home Office took over the direct reporting responsibility from the Prime Minister in 1952, while it is the Attorney General to whom

---

5 Interviews by Peter Chalk, Canberra, October 2007. See also Australian Security Intelligence Organisation (2006, p. 5) and "Australia to Double Spy Personnel," (2005).

6 Interview by Richard Warnes, October 2007.

ASIO reports, along with National Security Committee and Secretaries Committee on National Security.[7] In CSIS's case it is to the Inspector General (IG) of CSIS and, through the IG to the Minister of Public Safety and Emergency Preparedness (PSEP).[8] The BfV is answerable to the Minister of the Interior and subordinate to the *Bundesministerium Innern*, the Federal Ministry of the Interior.

In France, the DST is under the management and control of the French *Ministere de l'Interieur.* Within the Ministry, both the DST and the *Renseignements Generaux* or General Intelligence (very comparable to the Special Branch in Britain), which is to be absorbed by the DST—thus creating an organization mixing intelligence with police power—are controlled by *l'Inspection Generale de la Police Nationale.* For historical reasons, Sweden has a government of weak ministries and strong agencies. In these circumstances, the service reports to the Justice Ministry but is not managed day-to-day by the ministry. Rather, the service's activities are guided by a yearly "letter"—classified, in the service's case—from the ministry. The ministry exerts control through the budget and by setting quite general goals in the letter.

The use of intelligence's special sources entails special procedures in virtually all the countries. For instance, many of the DST's operations are instituted by enquiries into terrorism being carried out by the specialist *Juge d'Instruction* of the 14th *Section*, Paris, who specializes in Islamist terrorist investigations. In Britain, authority to use the various intelligence techniques is subject to the provisions of the Regulation of Investigatory Powers Act of 2000. The most intrusive techniques require personal authorization by a secretary of state, usually the Home Secretary, on a case demonstrating that the actions are necessary to protect national security, are proportionate to what they seek to achieve, and could not reasonably be obtained by other means. For CSIS, internal management controls reflect the agency's highly centralized char-

---

7 Interview by Peter Chalk, Canberra, November 2003. Burch (2007, p. 10); Department of the Prime Minister and Cabinet (Australia) (2006, p. 8).

8 Subsection 6(2) of the CSIS Act authorizes the PSEP to issue written directions to the service's Director—contained in a document known as the National Requirements for Security Intelligence—outlining where the agency should focus its investigative efforts and collection, analysis, and advisory priorities (Security Intelligence Review Committee, 2006, p. 36).

acter and consist of two committees, each of which is chaired by the service's Director—the Target and Approval and Review Committee and the Review Committee, which includes representatives from both the Justice and Public Safety departments as well as CSIS.

ASIO's intrusive measures—both human sources and communications intercepts—generally are undertaken in conjunction with the Australian Federal Police (AFP) and again need to be justified by strong reasons to believe the targets are actively engaged in activities threatening to national security and in all instances have to be initially supported by ASIO's Director General and subsequently sanctioned—on an individual basis, not in bundles—by the Attorney General.[9] In most cases, special powers have a mandated tenure of six months, after which the service must report in detail on how the powers were used and how they contributed to the investigation in question. In a new departure, ASIO is now empowered to obtain a Questioning Warrant from a federal magistrate that allows the agency to interrogate and, if necessary, hold the individual for up to 14 days without charge—a power that will sunset in 2016.

Organizational Structure and Funding Patterns

Virtually all of the organizations have had substantial funding increases since the turn of the millennium, as their staffing levels indicate. Although their domestic counterintelligence mission has waned, it has not gone away, and thus the dramatically increased prominence of the counterterrorism mission is, if not pure add-on, a substantial increase.

Structurally, most of the services have matrix organizations combining regions and functions. DST retains a largely functional structure, with directorates for counterespionage, international terrorism, protection of national assets, and the like. By contrast, CSIS revamped a similar structure in May 2006 to one that divides along geographic lines and consists of

---

[9] By contrast, AFP, a law enforcement organization, has to provide evidence that an individual has or is about to commit a crime before evoking its special powers (approval for which has to be granted by the Ombudsman) (interview by Peter Chalk, Canberra, October 2007).

- an International Branch, which deals with Sunni and Shi'ia extremism in Canada and overseas
- a Middle Eastern and Africa Branch, which primarily focuses on WMD proliferation concerns, both to groups and movements associated with global jihadist network and rogue regimes such as Iran
- an Asia, Americas, and Europe Branch, which addresses domestic extremism in Canada (the main emphasis being on right-wing and neo-Nazi militants), non-Islamic militant groups of concern (for instance, the LTTE) and Russian and Chinese activities aimed at stealing Canadian-patented or Canadian-sourced technology.[10]

The distinctive feature of the BfV is its network of state (*Land*) offices, comprising 16 *Landesamt für Verfassungsschutz* (LfVs) corresponding to the 16 *Länder* (states) of Germany, with independent authority for domestic intelligence and internal security within that *Land*. Once collated, evaluated, and interpreted by the BfV and the 16 LfVs, the resulting intelligence is entered into the organization's intelligence database, the *Nachrichtendienstlichen Informationssystem* (NADIS), which allows both access to the centralized intelligence and operational coordination between the central administration of the Federal BfV and the 16 regional LfVs, along with access by other German intelligence and police agencies.

Key Relationships with Intelligence and Law Enforcement Agencies

Not surprisingly, the agencies work most closely with kindred intelligence agencies and with national law enforcement partners. Also not surprisingly, while the links with law enforcement have always been there, the counterterrorism task has underscored them. Those links are very specifically spelled out in the British case, given the history of the police Special Branches and their mandate to do "covert intelligence work in relation to national security" and consequently assist the Security Service in "carrying out its statutory duties under the Security

---

[10] Interview by Peter Chalk, Washington D.C., June 2007.

Service Act 1989 [and] also support the work of the Secret Intelligence Service" (Home Office Communication Directorate, 2004).

ASIO and the AFP are tightly linked, and connections between CSIS and the RCMP are reinforced by the Integrated National Security Enforcement Teams, which were first established in 2002 in Vancouver, Montreal, Toronto, and Ottawa.[11] These task forces are made up of officers seconded from CSIS, RCMP, and relevant immigration and border control agencies.

As this report has emphasized, terrorism puts pressure on the seam between law enforcement and intelligence, in particular requiring decisions about when passive intelligence gathering should end and intervention begin. Britain, which had been thought by some experts to risk leaving groups on the street too long in order to collect more intelligence, has changed its policy. Now, if the risk of a terrorist act is deemed unacceptable, the police will intervene irrespective of the state of the evidence. The main operational consequence of this approach is that police detectives become involved far earlier in intelligence investigations being conducted by MI-5, perhaps in conjunction with Special Branch officers.

Cooperation in the French case is complicated by tension between DST and RG. The mandate and counterterrorist focus of the DST is predominantly foreign nationals posing a threat within France, while that of the RG is French nationals involved in internal subversion or "homegrown" terrorism. Technically, both organizations form part of the *Police Nationale*, under the control of the *Ministere de l'Interieur*, but there has been a history of duplication and rivalry, even outright hostility, between the two—perhaps an argument that if a nation is to have a domestic intelligence service, it should have only one.

On the positive side, the relationships in the intelligence world are promoted by interagency counterterrorism groups, especially for threat assessment. Most of these, which have remarkably similar names and acronyms, were established after 2001. Again, Britain is the prototype, with the Joint Threat Assessment Analysis Centre and the Centre for the Protection of National Infrastructure, both housed in MI-5 head-

---

[11] Interview by Peter Chalk, Washington D.C., June 2007.

quarters. Australia's counterparts are the National Counter-Terrorism Committee, created in October 2002, and the National Threat Assessments Centre, established in 2004; Canada's Integrated Threat Assessment Center, established in 2004, also sits at CSIS headquarters in Ottawa.

Oversight

Given the parliamentary structure of the governments in all the cases, none of the foreign services are subject to anything quite like congressional oversight in the United States, which can be led by the party *not* in control of the executive. In parliamentary systems, by definition, the majority party controls both the executive or government (prime minister and cabinet) and the legislature (parliament). Virtually all the countries have some form of oversight within the executive, plus some legislative committee. Not surprisingly, the powers of the executive overseers typically are more intrusive than those of the parliamentary committees, which are generally fairly modest, especially if the committees are "all-party," thus including opposition parties.

In Australia, for instance, the Attorney General's Inspector-General of Intelligence and Security and the Parliamentary Joint Committee on Intelligence and Security provide oversight. Given the circumstances of CSIS's founding, its oversight is particularly detailed, with two main external oversight entities for the agency—the Security and Intelligence Review Committee (SIRC) and the Inspector General (IG). Both are responsible to the Minister of Public Safety and Emergency Preparedness, who in turn is answerable to Parliament for the service as a whole. SIRC acts as an independent review agency, with a small, nonpartisan staff; it reports to the legislature and has a legal mandate to review the activities of CSIS. The IG functions as the "eyes and ears" of the PSEP.[12]

There is no parliamentary oversight of France's DST, a fact that is the historical legacy of having members of the French Communist Party (PCF) in governments during the Cold War, with the resulting

---

[12] Canadian Society for Industrial Security (2004); Security Intelligence Review Committee (2006, pp. 3, 32).

security concerns regarding their links to the Soviet Union. Nevertheless, though still weak, there is some level of judicial oversight of the DST, through the French system of *Juge*, while the main form of oversight is administrative, via the *Ministere de l'Interieur* and its *Comite Interministerial de Lutte Anti-Terrorist*, which provides a strategic and high-level oversight of the DST and counterterrorist coordination generally.

Metrics for Performance

Metrics for counterterrorism have been as elusive for these countries as for the United States. If they do systematic evaluation at all, most services fall back on evaluations, usually consumer surveys, of their outputs or major products. For instance, ASIO has attempted to come up with at least a rudimentary system for gauging performance, much of which is based on external feedback on its principal products. It, like CSIS, does not find those very valuable, not least because the return rate on surveys is usually low. Because customers are so diffuse in the domestic intelligence arena, they are especially hard to survey. For foreign intelligence, by contrast, while analysts may not be perfect judges of the value of collected information, they are at least regular and available judges. Still, when ASIO asked its customers to rank its advice and quality of analysis, roughly 98 percent ranked its almost always or generally useful (see Table 5.1).

Table 5.1
ASIO Client Survey Results, 2003–2005

	Almost Always Useful (%)		Generally Useful (%)		Sometimes Useful (%)		Rarely Useful (%)	
	2003–2004	2004–2005	2003–2004	2004–2005	2003–2004	2004–2005	2003–2004	2004–2005
Commonwealth	62.4	68	29.3	31	8.3	1	0	0
Police	66.5	57	29	40	4.5	3	0	0
Total (average)	64.5	62.5	29.2	35.5	6.4	2	0	0

SOURCE: Australian Security Intelligence Organisation (2005, p. 11).

The most concrete metrics for the services concern nonintelligence activities, such as security vetting, for which most of the services are responsible. CSIS, ASIO, and the Swedish service all provide security clearances for the national security portions of the government.

Scandals and Abuses

None of the services is a stranger to public dispute or scandal. Those tend to fall into three categories—penetrations of the service by hostile powers, usually the Soviet Union or, more recently, Russia; surveillance of political groups, especially on the left, that came to be deemed excessive; and perceived failures by the service and its fellow agencies to warn or act.

In the last category, for instance, the 1982 mid-air bombing of a Boeing 747 en route from Vancouver to Delhi killed all 329 on board—it was, until September 11, the worst case of airplane violence in history. The bombing, which was attributed to Sikh extremists based in Canada, led to an official board of inquiry whose final report in 2007 severely faulted CSIS (and the RCMP) for failing to act on information provided by police informers and the Indian Government that an attack was imminent.[13]

In the second category, CSIS was criticized more recently for failing to secure the release of Maher Arar, a Canadian citizen who was seized and secretly transported to Syria (the country of his birth) by American authorities while transiting New York in 2002. An official Commission of Inquiry reported in 2006 that Arar was imprisoned, interrogated, and tortured in a Damascus military intelligence facility for nearly a year. He has never been charged with any offense in Canada, the United States, or Syria. Although much of the focus was on the RCMP and damning but ultimately false information on Arar that it provided to the United States, the Commission also took issue with CSIS for failing to assess adequately the self-incriminating statements procured from Arar while in Syrian custody, especially whether

---

[13] "Canadian Agencies Were Warned of Air India in Attack," 2007; "Police Had Hint 11 Days Before 1985 Air India Bombing," 2007. For an in-depth account of the attack, see Jiwa (1987).

these were coerced through torture.[14] The Commission also faulted CSIS for failing to explicitly alert relevant authorities in the United States and Syria once it was clear that Arar did not represent a threat to Canadian national security.[15]

In France, concerns remain that existing "firewalls" in place prevent neither the intermixing of French domestic and external foreign intelligence nor the use of such intelligence by leading politicians to bolster their political arguments—in short, that intelligence is politicized. For instance, in 1973, DST telephone taps were discovered in the offices of the satirical left-wing magazine, *Le Canard Enchaine*. The resulting scandal and debates about spying for "political purposes" on other French nationals resulted in the resignation of the then Minister of the Interior (Porch, 1997).

Distrust of regular intelligence organizations by French politicians has impelled them to use parallel organizations. In perhaps the most extreme example, in 1982 President Mitterand established the "Elysee Cell" under the head of the *Gendarmerie Nationale* (GIGN), to lead the response to terrorism. This step caused significant concern because GIGN's primary mission was tactical intervention, rather than intelligence. Ultimately, allegations of false arrest and fabricated evidence emerged when three Irish nationals were arrested by the cell and accused of terrorism (Porch, 1997).

Lessons from Other Countries for the United States

National context matters enormously, especially in comparisons with the United States, whose population is more than three times larger than any of the six countries we examined and with a much more diverse federal system. That said, the reports on the arrangements of

[14] See Commission of Inquiry into the Actions of Canadian Officials in Relation to Maher Arar (2006, p. 13), Austen (2007a), and Austen (2007b).

[15] Commission of Inquiry into the Actions of Canadian Officials in Relation to Maher Arar (2006, p. 15).

six other countries suggest, first, several strengths of having a dedicated domestic service:

- Services with no functional law enforcement powers of arrest or detention devote the totality of their resources to preemptive information gathering, analysis, and dissemination.
- With no immediate requirement for prosecutions, the services can concentrate on long-term surveillance of terrorist suspects, trying to foster what might be called a "culture of prevention" with respect to terrorism.[16] For most of the services, threat assessments have been a major stock-in-trade, and several are the drivers of the interagency terrorism threat assessment process.
- The lack of police power may make it easier to develop community liaison, as the Australian and Canadian services, especially, have done. These activities not only give the services a more public face, they can be a "force multiplier" in enhancing the potential scope of national surveillance efforts by affording a direct way to assess the residual threat from home-grown extremists.
- They may be able to draw on a wider, more diverse pool of skills. More specifically, they are perhaps more able to attract people who would not normally be interested in entering a law enforcement profession, such as linguists, historians, social scientists, psychologists, economists, and country and regional experts.
- The division between intelligence and law enforcement has, perhaps somewhat paradoxically, compelled the creation of domestic coordinating mechanisms across that divide, which, in turn, has spurred the institution of wider, integrated antiterrorism planning. Rather than blurring the "wall," the continued separation requires agencies who work on both sides of it to understand in detail the requirements and working habits of the other side.

To be sure, it is hard to judge how much of this is the effect of having separate police and intelligence agencies and how much it stems from smaller size and from longer history. For instance, Brit-

---

16 See, for instance, U.S. General Accounting Office (2002a, p. 8).

ish arrangements are often regarded as quite impressive, involving substantial interagency cooperation that has earned the nickname "Britain Counterterrorism Inc." Yet while the core may be a domestic intelligence service without police power, British cooperation stems from a nearly 40-year history of dealing with terrorists in Northern Ireland, in England, and abroad.

Perhaps the most relevant experience is that of America's immediate neighbor, Canada. Like the FBI, its Royal Canadian Mounted Police combined policing and intelligence. Very much in parallel with the FBI's COINTELPRO, it turned out that the RCMP Security Service had harassed the separatist Parti Québécois in a variety of ways, from stealing its mail and breaking into its offices, to engaging in illegal eavesdropping, to burning a barn in which the Black Panther Party and Front de Libération du Québec were rumored to be planning to meet. In response, a royal commission, the McDonald Commission, investigated and recommended creating a separate intelligence service. The Canadian Security and Intelligence Service began operating in 1984. In effect, the United States and Canada had come to the same pass, both realizing that their domestic security arms had imposed their own view of what the nation's security implied, but then divided over what to do. For the United States, the solution was the famous "wall"; for Canada, it was a separate service. The primary argument for creating CSIS was a legal one: to have clear legislation and detailed oversight. But a secondary argument had to do with effectiveness: absent major terror or a spy scandal, the Security Service would lose out in the internal competition for resources to the Mounties' main law enforcement mission. It was likely to suffer a boom-and-bust cycle as terrorism and spying rose and fell on the public's agenda of concern.

If the United States were to contemplate a domestic intelligence service, the organization of the German service, the BfV, would be a suggestive model. So might the regional offices of the French domestic service. Regional BfV offices in each *Land* (state) responsible for domestic intelligence and internal security within are linked to and report back to the federal BfV in Cologne. Indeed, such a devolution of authority would be all the more necessary given the very different circumstances in different parts of the United States; that is suggested by the 56 FBI field offices (and 400 resident agencies) that already exist in the United States. In principle, the BfV's single NADIS database is also suggestive, though from outside it is hard to judge how well it actually works. It provides a repository for all information and intelligence from the various regional BfV as well as BfV headquarters could provide, and it does so in a way that is both secure and accessible to appropriate officials at the local level.

The principal negative from the experiences of other countries is that, for all the various initiatives, integrating intelligence and law enforcement in the fight against terror remains a parlous enterprise. Surely, having a separate service is no panacea for interagency conflict: Britain's domestic service, MI-5, and its police Special Branch argued for years over which would take the lead against terrorism outside Northern Ireland. Operationally, how to collect information for evidentiary purposes while simultaneously protecting both the identity of covert sources and the secrecy of surveillance and monitoring methods remains a problem. Tactical intelligence for immediate law enforcement purposes is very different from strategic intelligence about threats. The difference is reflected in the inherent tension between continuing to gather intelligence on suspicious activity, on the one hand, and rolling up that activity through law enforcement (or other disruption) on the other.

In that sense, the foreign comparisons also illustrate the advantages to the FBI hybrid model in quickly translating covert information into actionable law enforcement purposes, its case-based culture notwithstanding. There may be benefit to having one agency deal with particular cases, using "case" broadly, from "grain to bread," as the Swedish service puts it. Surely, the creation of a domestic intelligence agency, whatever its merits, cannot in of itself address the larger problem of data coordination and sharing outside its organizational ambit.[17] Note that the London and Madrid attacks occurred in countries that did have a separate service. Even if such a service were better able to

---

[17] See Burch (2007, p. 3) and Taylor (2004, p. 64).

characterize the threat, the connection between characterizing it and preventing it is not direct.[18]

By the same token, another critical question—whether systems for oversight and accountability are more effective with a separate domestic intelligence service—is difficult to disentangle from history, culture, and size. There might be advantages to having a separate service overseen entirely in terms of intelligence rather than as part of a larger law enforcement organization. The relatively broad latitude the "letter" system gives the Swedish FBI-like service might be seen as support of that point, but, again, the difference probably derives more from the basic nature of Swedish government. On the other hand, the lack of any effective parliamentary oversight over France's service could be seen as a separate service's successful quest for more autonomy. However, again, that lack of oversight probably has more to with the specifics of the French case and with Cold War concerns over Communists in government than with anything inherent in fashioning a separate domestic intelligence service.

What we have called the exploratory function of domestic intelligence entails collecting data to be analyzed then stored for potential future use. As has been illustrated by countless incidents of identity theft, Americans understand the risks of compromised personal data. Whether such information is more secure in the hands of many different law enforcement and intelligence organizations, protected according to individual agency rules, or whether it is safer stored centrally, perhaps under better and more consistent protections—but more readily available for those seeking to assemble and analyze the data, and perhaps offering one large "honey pot" target—these are issues that the foreign comparisons cannot settle.

Moreover, the context of all the countries we examined is not only less federal than that of the United States, it also tends to be one in which citizens are generally less skeptical of their governments and more inclined to defer to its powers. The point should not be overstated, but Australia, which often seems closer to the United States than continental Europe, speaks to it. In Australia, the enabling act empowers

---

18 See, for instance, Burch (2007 pp. 18–19).

the service's director general both to decide the strategic direction of the agency and to determine what constitutes a legitimate target for surveillance. Moreover, since 2003 the service has had a limited right to interrogate and hold terrorist suspects without charging them with a specific offense.[19] Taken together, these provisions have effectively led to the emergence of an intelligence service that can not only task itself but also authorize itself.

Mission, Function, and Organization

Against these comparisons from abroad, consider the concerns set out in Table 3.1, the ones that are driving the issue of whether to create a separate domestic intelligence agency in the United States. The first—that the FBI is and is destined to remain dominated by law enforcement and a case-based approach—is about *mission and function* and the processes that flow from that mission. All the other concerns are about *process.* For the first, which is really the core issue in thinking about whether to create a new service, the organizational questions are two: first, are efforts, like those currently underway, to reshape the mission and processes of the FBI doomed to fail (and how would we know); and, second, if so, would creating a new organization actually produce the outcomes sought (and how would we know)?

In addressing those questions, the lines of organization theory on *strategic choice* and *competitive strategy* are only tangentially relevant.[20] Private organizations have more scope for strategic choice than government agencies typically do, for they can choose in which marketplaces to compete and can create new products and market niches. Moreover, private-sector executives have the discretion to buy, sell, or eliminate components of the firm to fulfill the objectives of powerful stakeholders. Still, this perspective does direct attention to organizational design

---

[19] Telephone interview by Peter Chalk, June 2007.

[20] The now-classic work is Michael Porter, *Competitive Advantage*, New York: Free Press, New York, 1985.

and effectiveness and, especially, to the constraints in the operating environment.

Because most public-sector organizations lack a handy bottom line, clarity in mission is critical. That clarity provides a reason for thinking about a separate domestic intelligence agency. The Volcker Commission, formally the National Commission on the Public Service, emphasized the need for missions that are clear and unambiguous (Volcker Commission, 2003).[21] *Government Executive*'s examination of five years of reviews of agencies' performance did so as well (Treverton, 2004). High-performing agencies begin with missions that are clear and clearly supported by Congress. For instance, the Social Security Administration's mission is to get checks and information to people who need them. By contrast, the old Immigration and Naturalization Service (INS) and the Forest Service ranked poorly in part because their missions were split—for INS, to keep illegal immigrants out of the United States *and* to help legal immigrants become citizens and receive federal benefits; for the Forest Service, to preserve public lands *and* produce resources from them. Organizations that arose in fairly direct response to political pressure are especially likely to have split missions (Lewis, 2003).

By this line of reasoning, the question is whether a transformed FBI whose mission was intelligence-driven prevention would in fact have the clarity of a single mission. While law enforcement can certainly be a tool in prevention, it remains to be proven that the historical tensions between law enforcement and intelligence can be resolved when both are in the service of a prevention mission. The experiences of the foreign services we assessed suggested the value of a single focus on prevention, with the intelligence collection and analysis to support it. Perhaps the single greatest teething pain of DHS—which brought together 180,000 employees from 22 existing agencies—has been that the constituent agencies did not, and still do not, share a single mission (far from it). By one rule of thumb, the constituent agencies in a merger like DHS ought to overlap in mission by at least half.

---

[21] However, a major focus of the commission was on the creation of DHS, which is perhaps not the best example of an agency with an unambiguous mission.

The history of organizational design in the public sector is cautionary in that, in contrast to the rational choices to maximize profit that are presumed to be at the root of private-sector design, it shows that public-sector organizational design is a political process of competition among interests and interest groups. In the words of one of the classic works: "American public bureaucracy is not designed to be effective. The bureaucracy arises out of politics, and its design reflects the interests, strategies, and compromises of those who exercise political power" (Moe, 1989, p. 267). By this line of argument, the more a particular interest group succeeds in shaping an organization to its tastes, the more it will want to insulate that organization from future politics—for instance, by making it an independent agency, rather than part of a departmental hierarchy, by emphasizing professionalism, and by increasing the control of career officials (and limiting that of political appointees).

In contrast, those who regard themselves as "losers" in the agency's design will have the opposite preference, seeking to open it to future politics and thus to reshuffled priorities, even missions. The interests of presidents run roughly in parallel to the extent they regard themselves as responsible for effective governance. Looking to their place in history, they will have their own agendas and their own grander view about what is best for society, or at least large chunks of it. Thus, they will look for ways to impose their agenda and view on agencies, not insulate those agencies.

The interests at issue in decisions about intelligence are less pecuniary, hence less immediately visible, than those involving agencies such as the Department of Agriculture or the Forest Service. Yet they are still powerful. In that sense, the pre–September 11 separation of law enforcement and intelligence suited a disparate combination of interests. It played to the FBI's historic mission and identity and to the stakes of local authorities that wanted federal help in fighting crime. At the same time, it offered groups that worried about civil liberties the promise that domestic intelligence would be limited and that most federal investigation would be done within the strictures of law enforcement cases.

By emphasizing the politics of organizational design, this line of reasoning helps explain why reorganizations in government so often seem to fail. It thus suggests a certain indeterminacy about what a domestic intelligence service actually would look like, should one be created. If it were legislated in the wake of another major attack, with the body politic frightened and permissive, a president might get what he or she sought, for better or for worse. If it were created in more normal circumstances, the result would be political compromise. The resulting agency might not reflect exactly what any participant in the process sought, and it might combine a mission and constraints on carrying out that mission that could raise questions about whether it was an effective response to the organizational concerns that it was created to address.

How insulated or open the organizational outcome was from future political influences would turn on a clutch of details, which would themselves be the result of compromises in the political arena. Insulation comes in many forms.[22] If the authorizing legislation were written in very specific terms, that would tie the hands of future officials in the organization—or insulate them from future pressures, depending on one's view of the outcome. The more independence a new agency had, the more autonomy it would have in shaping and sustaining its mission. In that sense, the scale of increasing autonomy would run from the current FBI National Security Branch, to something like the Branch but with more statutory autonomy, to a new agency with a relationship to DOJ similar to the relationship that the FBI currently has with DOJ, to, conceivably, an independent agency.

In this light, if the new agency were located in some departmental hierarchy, it would surely matter which one: Being in Justice would make it part of an established organization dominated by law enforcement, whereas a location in DHS would subject it to the pressures of a work in progress, one now dominated by border control and crisis management. Similarly, how many political appointees the agency had and whether they were appointed for fixed terms would also matter. The FBI is a very closed professional service, one dominated by its

[22] Lewis (2003, p. 8 on).

agents, with only a single political appointee—the director—and that appointee has a fixed, ten-year term. Until recently, lateral movements into the Bureau's senior managerial ranks were rare, and even now they are driven by needs for technical or management expertise, not politics. These questions would all be important for a new agency, as would the height and width of the agency's hierarchy, the agency's latitude in selecting and training the professionals that would compose it, and a host of other details.

Structure and Process[23]

This perspective on organizational design in the public sector suggests, in effect, how the political arena will shape outcomes with regard to *structure,* the dimensions of which run back to Max Weber nearly a century ago:[24] How are the organization's work units and their roles located and distributed; how centralized is the organization; how formalized in its rules and procedures; how standardized are its various jobs; how much horizontal specialization is there across work groups; and how much vertical specialization in a hierarchy that distributes formal authority?

Organizational structures can be characterized in a number of ways, all of which now recognize that information needs are a key driver against the nature of the external environment. One characterization is historical, noting the evolution, especially in the private sector, from simple, centralized structures to division-based structures after World War II, to matrix organizations and horizontal ones by the 1990s, to the most decentralized, or modular, forms more recently.[25]

Another characterization is perhaps more suggestive for both a possible domestic intelligence agency and the larger domestic intel-

---

[23] We are grateful to, and have drawn from the work of our colleague, Lynn Scott, in this analysis. It also draws on a draft prepared by the Program on National Security Reform (no date).

[24] His 1922 classic is reprinted as "Bureaucracy" in Shafritz and Hyde (1992).

[25] See, for instance, Daft (2004).

ligence enterprise. It distinguishes three types—front end/back end, functional integrator, and distributed organization (Galbraith, 1995). The front/back type characterizes the traditional view of government intelligence organizations, with a "product" assembly side producing intelligence and a distribution (or dissemination) side interacting with the customers. For intelligence, the canonical intelligence "cycle"—requirements, collection, analysis, dissemination—was the bridge between products and the needs of consumers.

The functional integrator organization is more a way of coordinating across organizations than a specific type of organizational structure, and in that sense it is probably more suggestive for the broader domestic intelligence enterprise than for a specific federal agency. The central idea is a mirror-image structure, in which units have similar functional divisions. For the domestic intelligence enterprise, this might emphasize the role of the center—either a new domestic service or the existing FBI—as the model or standard-setter. Other organizations in the domestic intelligence enterprise (federal, state, or local) might shape their processes and practices of collection and analysis on that model and against its standards.

The third type, distributed organization, takes the analysis into process, for it imagines coequal headquarters (for intelligence, perhaps, read "organizations") that coordinate activities. It relies heavily on reciprocal processes among units. *Reciprocal* processes put a premium on fast and informal communications, especially across units, and on teamwork. Ideally, the units would be colocated, as well as tightly linked in communication, though the colocation in the future may be virtual, not physical. In any case, the sense of joint responsibility across units needs to be high, along with the ability of individuals to respond rapidly both to each other and to changes in external circumstances. As suggested in more detail below, this is a good description for the goal of what is called "information sharing" in the wider domestic intelligence enterprise.

Distinct from reciprocal processes, *pooled* processes rely heavily on standard operating procedures; information needs across units are low and so is the requirement for colocation. Policing is essentially a pooled process, but given the enormous discretion of police on the beat, law enforcement organizations have always struggled with both formalization and standardization. The results have been rules aplenty—efforts to build and make institutional standard operating procedures, along with oversight mechanisms, such as police commissions.

Sequential processes, like assembly lines or task forces, depend on planning, scheduling, and periodic feedback. As a result, they imply a lesser need for communication and colocation than do reciprocal processes. Task forces can meet from time to time to discuss what they've done and to decide both on next steps and on who or which group will do them. In one sense, the traditional intelligence cycle could be conceived as a sequential process, though with the recognition that the planning might be short-circuited at any time by new information or pressing consumer demands.

Both structure and process need to be adapted to the environment in which the organization must operate, for outcomes will depend on how good the fit is between the structures and processes that make up the organization, or enterprise, and the characteristics of its operating environment. The external environment usually is characterized along similar dimensions, for example:[26]

- *Generosity:* The capacity of the environment to sustain organizational growth and stability. Here, the environment for domestic intelligence has been generous since September 11. Concern is frequently expressed, though, about what will ensue if another major terrorist attack does not occur.
- *Dynamism:* Changes in the environment that are hard to predict. The environment of the domestic intelligence enterprise surely is dynamic. New terrorist groups and new attack modes will arise.
- *Complexity:* The number of relevant actors and components in the environment; the difference in operating domains of the organization; and the interdependence the focal organization has with other organizations in the environment. As stressed again and again, complexity is the hallmark of domestic intelligence.

---

[26] Among many, see, for instance, Daft (2004) and Huber Daft (1987).

- *Uncertainty:* The relative difference between the amount of information required to perform its tasks and the amount actually possessed by the organization. High uncertainty in this dimension is also characteristic of domestic intelligence. We can't be sure what we don't know, and what we don't know may kill us (Galbraith, 1973).

Traditional models that featured standard operating procedures and specialization are harder pressed to cope when operating environments become increasingly uncertain, complex, dynamic, or ungenerous. Notice, for instance, the contrast between traditional law enforcement and counterterrorism. While crime involved many organizations, there was considerable horizontal specialization: At the federal level, different agencies specialized in different kinds of crime—drugs, or firearms, or organized crime—and responsibility for different crimes was parceled out among federal, state, and local organizations.

The fight against terror, by contrast, introduces dramatic new elements of dynamism, complexity, and uncertainty. Its complexity, for instance, breaks down both horizontal and vertical specialization; it may be more important to get a particular piece of information to the infrastructure manager on the front lines than it is to get it to the President of the United States. Moreover, none of the traditional responses to increased uncertainty—for instance, creating self-contained subunits with specific functional responsibilities—are really relevant to the campaign against terror.

Rather, newer information-processing models suggest that organizations will seek to develop information systems for gathering information at points of origin, performing analysis, and directing customized information to any number of decisionmakers in the hierarchy. For the domestic intelligence enterprise, "information-sharing" initiatives are almost a perfect analogy to this guidance, seeking to collect and analyze information at many points in the enterprise and to get that information to many decisionmakers when they need it. The analogy extends still further, for recent research suggests that better information systems still may not mitigate all of the negative characteristics of the environment. Productive organization redesign options then will most likely take one of three courses—changing structural components, introducing or expanding information systems, or an integration of both strategies.

The propositions from organization theory do not directly prescribe whether to create a separate intelligence service or how much it should coordinate information flows within the broader domestic intelligence enterprise. But they are suggestive. Creating a separate intelligence service without law enforcement powers would be a structural response to increased dynamism and uncertainty, seeking to create capacity to scan for new threats and to ask continually what it is that the organization should know but doesn't.

From Traditional Process to Sensemaking

In looking closer at decisionmaking processes, traditional organization theory applied two criteria to decisions: How fast are they, and how comprehensive are they—that is, are all relevant factors pertaining to the decision included in the process? The rub is that the criteria are often at odds with each other. Fast decisions often come at the cost of comprehensiveness, and vice versa. Moreover, these criteria for decisions also bear on the design of organizations. In traditional organizations, fast decisions tended to be associated with a decentralized authority structure and fewer hierarchical levels between the operating levels of the organization and executives (Eisenhardt, 1989). The pre–September 11 FBI was such an organization. Its field offices were located where the crimes were committed, and each office had considerable autonomy.

By contrast, comprehensive decisions imply information processing and vetting through the hierarchy to a centralized decision authority. Most government decisions most of the time are comprehensive in that they need to reflect many factors and many stakeholders. National Intelligence Estimates and other forms of analysis seek to be comprehensive, though they are not decisions. In the traditional view, organizations that require comprehensive processes should maintain hierarchical structures or build information systems that can handle more information than the hierarchy is able to process.

Again, in the traditional view, if an organization operates in an environment of high dynamism, then it should be able to make fast decisions. That calls for information processes that can sort out the critical information; the law enforcement preoccupation with information that is relevant to a particular case is such a sorting mechanism. Limiting hierarchical structure can also keep decisions as close to operations as possible.

Finally, complex environments present unique challenges to organizations because they require decisionmaking processes that are both comprehensive and fast. Partners, competitors, rules of engagement, political stakeholders, and the geography of different operating locations all represent different points of view and different kinds of information that needed to be integrated in making decisions—an apt characterization of the domestic intelligence enterprise. As a result, the traditional guidance to organizations was a combination of vertically specialized hierarchy to match the complexity of information processing and decentralized decision making to make fast decisions close to operations.

Table 5.2 summarizes these considerations, with examples relevant to domestic intelligence.

It was the particular challenges of dealing with high complexity—exactly the circumstances of the fight against terror—that led to another line of thinking about organization and especially about process: sensemaking.[27] That approach was spurred by looking at major failures, such as the Three Mile Island nuclear accident or the space shuttle *Challenger* disaster.[28] These examinations sought to understand how complexity "could blind people to emerging catastrophes or create vicious cycles that could lead to major failures in crises" (Program on National Security Reform, no date). In that sense, although the pre–September 11 FBI was very well shaped for law enforcement—decentralized into geographically defined units, with a flat hierarchy and thus the abil-

---

[27] The term derives from Weick (1995).

[28] See, for instance, Perrow (1984) and Weick and Sutcliffe (2001).

Table 5.2
Operating Environments, Decision Requirements, and Design Considerations

Salient Characteristic of Operating Environment	Decision Requirement	Design Considerations	Example Relevant to Domestic Intelligence
High uncertainty	Comprehensive	Vertical specialization Decentralization IT to collect, analyze	National Intelligence Estimates
High dynamism	Fast	Limit hierarchy IT to share vertically and horizontally	FBI law enforcement
High complexity	Fast and comprehensive	Maintain vertical specialization Decentralization IT to analyze, scan, synthesize	Intelligence across the entire domestic enterprise

ity to make decisions fast—it and its fellow organizations were not designed for the complex environment of the terrorist threat.

The first approaches to knowledge management tended to treat knowledge as something that could be transferred, kept, used, and reused—in short, *learned*; sensemaking treats knowledge in social terms as something that has to be created, is difficult to move across organizational and other boundaries ("sticky"), is "'recontextualized' in moving from one context to another," can decay or be destroyed, and has to "be 'reaccomplished' from day to day" (Program on National Security Reform, no date). Under the sensemaking approach, information is less learned by the organization than *created* by it. Again, the view is not directly prescriptive, but it is highly suggestive. The language of "information sharing" dominates current discussion of the wider domestic intelligence enterprise. Yet from a sensemaking perspective, the goal is not sharing information but jointly *creating* it across federal, state, local, and private organizations.[29]

The sensemaking perspective is also suggestive for more fine-grain processes within individual agencies and across the domestic

29 Lt. John Sullivan of the Los Angeles County Sheriff's Department refers to this process as "coproduction."

intelligence enterprise, especially analytic processes as they encounter the complexity of the terrorist threat. The stream of events is likely to include some disruptive "environmental jolts" that when identified for further attention can trigger a process of "sense-losing."[30] Thus, in sensemaking, the aim is to help groups move from what seems to them order, to the chaos of disruption, and then to build a new order.

In shaping those processes, the watchwords are[31]

- **Social:** People don't discover sense, they create it, usually in conversations. Those conversations are critical.
- **Identity:** The first identities that surface in an inexplicable event, identities such as "victim" or "fighter," lock people in to overly limited options. Moving beyond first identities is imperative.
- **Retrospect:** Faced with the inexplicable, people often act their way out of their puzzlement by talking and looking at what they have said in order to discover what they may be thinking. The need is to make it possible for people to talk their way from the superficial, through the complex, on to the profound.
- **Cues:** People deal with the inexplicable by paying attention to a handful of cues that enable them to construct a larger story. They look for cues that confirm their analysis; and in doing so, they ignore a great deal. Expanding the range and variety of cues is important.
- **Ongoing:** Sensemaking is dynamic and requires continuous updating and reaccomplishment. Groups cannot languish in thinking, "Now we have it figured out."
- **Plausibility:** What is unsettling when people face the inexplicable is that they tend to treat any old explanation as better than nothing. That is healthy, but the first plausible account cannot be the last possible story.
- **Enactment:** Most of all, in inexplicable times, people have to keep moving. Recovery lies not in thinking then doing, but in

30 See Meyer (1982) and Orton (2000).

31 See Weick (1995) and Weick (no date). The watchwords and their descriptions listed here are partial quotes or are paraphrased from the latter.

thinking while doing and in thinking by doing. People need to keep moving and paying attention.

The watchwords are abstract, but they suggest the goals both in designing organizations and especially in fashioning processes within and across them. *Mindfulness* is critical, both in the sense of being open-minded but also in the sense of being aware of just how uncertain the complexity of reality can be and how possible it is that the group will be surprised. Suppose, for instance, that the FBI and CIA officers who met in New York in June 2001 had engaged in a sensemaking conversation, instead of mutually holding back information they weren't sure they could pass to each other. They might have led to the joint discovery of where two of the September 11 terrorists were. Broadened, it might have introduced flight schools as a jolt, which might then have triggered another round of conversation in an effort to make some sense of that inexplicable piece.

Forms of a "New Domestic Intelligence Agency"

"Create a new domestic intelligence agency" can mean quite different things. In light of the discussion of organization structure and process, this analysis focuses on the two most straightforward alternatives. The first alternative is to assemble parts of existing agencies to create a separate agency, one with about the same relationship to the Department of Justice that the FBI currently has. The second alternative is to create an "agency within an agency" in the FBI or perhaps DHS. The Gilmore Commission in 2004 recommended a version of the first alternative, involving the transfer of staff from the CIA, FBI, and other relevant organizations (Gilmore Commission, 2002, pp. iii–iv). This alternative would seek to simplify the current complexity of the domestic intelligence enterprise, but the transition costs would be high in terms of short-term disruption as the current enterprise was taken apart and reassembled.

One form of the "agency within an agency" might be a more autonomous version of the National Security Branch of the FBI. The

Commission on the Intelligence Capabilities of the United States Regarding Weapons of Mass Destruction (the "WMD Commission") recommended the creation of a "National Security Service" within the FBI, but "subject to the coordination and budget authorities of the DNI" (WMD Commission, 2005, p. 451).

If it remained at the FBI, the agency-within-an-agency would involve less short-term disruption than creating a stand-alone agency. How much it differed from what is now being built in the FBI National Security Branch would be driven by decisions about how autonomous it should be in pursuing its intelligence mission. *Who* was recruited and *how* they were trained and rewarded would be matters of great consequence. Already the Executive Assistant Director for the National Security Branch has considerable autonomy—for instance, the authority to allocate resources based on threat, although that authority has not yet been used in allocating intelligence analysts (DOJ OIG, 2007b).

As the countries with a separate service report, they feel they have two distinct advantages that bear on human resources. First, with no immediate requirement for prosecutions, the services can concentrate on long-term surveillance of terrorist suspects, trying to foster what might be called a "culture of prevention" with respect to political extremism.[32] And second, they may be able to draw on a wider, more diverse recruitment pool. More specifically, they are perhaps more able to attract individuals who would not normally be interested in entering a law enforcement profession, such as linguists, historians, social scientists, psychologists, economists, and country and regional experts.

The challenge for a new service, as for other intelligence organizations, would be to construct metrics that measure *outputs*, if not *outcomes*. In law enforcement, relevant metrics are at hand: Arrests and convictions can be see as *outputs*, which can be seen as leading to what really matters, the *outcome* of safer streets. The problem for intelligence is that connections between intelligence outputs—such as reports written or warnings sounded—and outcomes are very indirect. For counterterrorism intelligence in particular, the challenge is harder still, for the outcome sought is no terror attacks. The challenge for a new service,

---

[32] See, for instance, U.S. General Accounting Office (2002a, p. 8).

as for the FBI now, is to devise ways of indirectly measuring the contribution of intelligence—in some combination of internal assessments and external judgments of value—as a surrogate for outcome measures. Those would then serve as a basis for how analysts were rewarded, both formally and informally.

As in other areas of public policy, and life, the devil would be in the details in shaping a new agency, as other experiences with government reorganizations have made all too apparent. First, where should it be located? Here, either DOJ or DHS would be a logical choice. If the new agency were in DOJ, with about the same relationship to the department as the FBI has today, it should find it easier to work across the federal intelligence–law enforcement seam with its colleagues in the FBI. On the other hand, it would still be housed in a preeminently law enforcement organization. A home at DHS would place it close to embedded collectors, such as the Coast Guard and TSA, and would reinforce the "homeland" focus of the intelligence organization. On the other hand, DHS already more than has its hands full sorting out its current constituent parts, which argues against adding a new one.

Second, if a new agency were assembled out of existing pieces, which pieces should be selected? Most of the FBI National Security Branch would be a natural choice, but what about DHS Office of Intelligence Analysis? Including it would seem logical, especially if the new agency were to have a primary mandate for reaching out to state and local partners. Yet if it were not housed at DHS, taking the Office of Intelligence Analysis would either leave DHS without an in-house intelligence organization or, more likely, impel it to create a new one. And what about CIA's National Resources Division? That has a network of stations across the United States that the new service could use as the basis for its own infrastructure. Currently, Natural Resources debriefs travelers and serves as a base for other collection operations aimed abroad. But including it would bespeak the need to build connections across the domestic-foreign divide even as the nation created a new "domestic" service.

What about NCTC? For most of America's foreign partners, the domestic service is the primary coordinator for counterterrorism intelligence. That is true of Australia's National Threat Assessment Centre,

Britain's Joint Threat Assessment Centre (which is collocated with MI-5), and Canada's Integrated Threat Assessment Center. Currently, NCTC works for the DNI in its intelligence function. Moving it to a new agency, or colocating it there, would make sense if, again, that agency were to be the primary vehicle for sharing information downward across the federal system. On the other hand, the birth pains of a new domestic intelligence agency, especially in the context of the United States, which has never had one, might narrow the focus and performance of NCTC.

Finally, what about the dotted lines on organization charts of the U.S. intelligence enterprise, which suggest informal relationships between agencies—or the relationships that do not appear at all on such charts but are important in actual practice? The history of the DNI since 2004 has been one of conflict with the main intelligence agencies over what the DNI's statutory authorities—in most cases more than consultation but less than command—mean about appointments, personnel policies, and the like. In the case of a new agency, how much of a lead would a new agency have in coordinating domestic intelligence collection, or in reaching out to state and local authorities? Would it set standards for producing information and moving it around the entire domestic intelligence enterprise? If so, how would it enforce those standards? Or would those functions reside with the DNI?

Our interviews suggested there is value in having a separate agency reaching out to, and perhaps setting standards for, for instance, the military agencies engaged in domestic intelligence, such as the Naval Criminal Investigative Service (NCIS) and the Counterintelligence Field Activity (CIFA). CIFA, set up in the wake of September 11, came under criticism when it was disclosed that it had collected information on antiwar protesters after the 2003 invasion of Iraq, and it was to be disbanded in 2008, with its personnel integrated into the Defense Intelligence Agency. In any case, the force and meaning of those dotted lines and of the even more informal relationships across the domestic intelligence enterprise would be important. They might also be contentious.

CHAPTER SIX

Weighing Pros and Cons: An Approach for Considering the Uncertain Costs and Benefits of Organizational Change

A systematic examination of the pros and cons of making organizational changes to domestic intelligence activities can provide some insight into how creating a new agency might affect both the ability of the country to prevent terrorist attack and public concern about the effects of intelligence on the nation more broadly. However, doing so provides no clear *answer* on the advisability of such a reorganization. How much creating a new agency will actually reduce the risk of terrorist attack compared with the current structure of domestic intelligence activities is unknown.[1] Whether a reorganization would create more efficient oversight or, conversely, result in broader concerns about government infringement on privacy and civil liberties is hard to predict *a priori*.

Quite simply, the potential value depends on too many things, ranging from assumptions about how well the reorganization could be done to the scope of the threat that domestic intelligence efforts are intended to address. Some of the uncertainties are created by the lack of information that could better inform a choice, while others are driven by personal preferences that will cause the apparent value of creating a separate domestic agency to differ from one person to another.

[1] A similar point has been made by Hammond (2007) in assessing problems with evaluating changes in structure for the intelligence community overall.

As a result of the uncertainties, the decision of whether to create a new domestic counterterrorism intelligence agency is less a matter of adding up the pros and cons to reach a clear policy decision than it is a question of how to make choices in the absence of certain information. Alternative approaches are needed that make it possible to see how the decision might vary if different assumptions are made. To that end, we applied a framework called "break-even analysis," developed specifically for situations where great uncertainty surrounds the benefits associated with a policy or regulatory choice. RAND has previously applied this methodology to the analysis of homeland security policies.[2]

A break-even analysis, using the general structure of cost-benefit analysis, provides a way to consider how the benefits and costs—or pros and cons—of a policy change compare and how the balance between them might shift when different assumptions are made about the security environment, the effects of an intelligence reorganization, and other factors.[3] In contrast to approaches that try to reach a single answer as to whether a policy change would be beneficial,[4] this approach compares the potentially uncertain costs and benefits to explore the question: How good would a domestic intelligence agency *have to be* to warrant creating it? Conducting this type of analysis requires returning to the varied costs and benefits associated with founding a new agency that have been alluded to throughout this report, thinking through both their potential magnitude and how they might vary depending on how the organization was created.

Considering Costs

Some costs that would be associated with creating a new agency are relatively tangible, such as the basic organizational costs. As a benchmark, the total FBI budget for 2008 is $6.4 billion; the portion allo-

---

2 See LaTourrette and Willis (2007) for a discussion.

3 Such an approach is similar to reported deliberations at the Office of Management and Budget in the Executive Office of the President in 2003 discussed in Skrzycki (2003) and Andrews (2003).

4 For example, a judgment that the costs of creating a new agency are justified by the benefits of doing so under a specific set of assumptions.

cated to the strategic goal of preventing terrorism and promoting the nation's security, which includes both the Bureau's counterterrorism and counterintelligence activities, is $3.8 billion.[5] In principle, if the entire National Security Branch, along with other government elements, were simply transferred to a new agency, the additional annual cost to the nation could be relatively small. There would still be, however, the costs of buildings and infrastructure, new personnel systems, and training—of these costs, some would be paid only once when the agency was created and others would be recurring costs. Moreover, past experience suggests that while moving entire agencies is messy enough, attempts to move only parts are likely to meet with resistance from the old agency. Less will be transferred than expected, the old agency will shrink by less than anticipated, and the new agency will grow. Any functions that were transferred only "in part" or were reconstituted in the old agency after the new one was created can be viewed as additional annual costs associated with creating the new organization compared with the status quo. An "agency-within-an agency" plainly would be cheaper, especially if it were built out of the National Security Branch in the FBI.

Yet any new agency would still need new some offices and infrastructure, new personnel systems and training facilities, and the like. In particular, a new agency either would or would not inherit the JTTFs and other infrastructure, both physical and human, for reaching out to state and local authorities. If it did not, then it would have to build that infrastructure; if it did, the FBI would have to re-create it for law enforcement purposes. Implementation of new personnel systems could have additional costs, illustrated by the litigation regarding efforts to change personnel policies at the Department of Defense and the Department of Homeland Security (Lee, 2006). If entirely new data systems were viewed as necessary to bring together intelligence data in a new agency, the costs associated with its design, procurement,

---

[5] These are FBI numbers (see Federal Bureau of Investigation, 2007, pp. 1–3). Any allocation of budgets by function is somewhat arbitrary, so this number is at best suggestive of what the FBI spends on "counterterrorism."

and operation could be considerable.[6] If a new agency were viewed as requiring exemption from current civil service ways of operation—for instance, having the ability to pay analysts more to attract and keep them—then these would represent additional annual costs.

Examples of cost estimates for government reorganizations are available that could guide thinking about what the creation of a new intelligence organization might cost: For example, the Congressional Budget Office estimated that the costs associated with the reorganization of the agencies and the administrative costs involved in creating DHS would range from $225 million to $240 million annually. If the formation of a new agency resulted in broader changes in program or the creation of new capabilities (e.g., procurement of new computer systems to manage intelligence information), costs could be significantly higher, though such additions are not directly related to the specific organizational structure of intelligence activities (Congressional Budget Office, 2002).

Other costs that have been discussed throughout this report are more elusive—for instance, the less tangible costs of making the transition to new arrangements and, especially, potential costs to privacy or civil liberties.[7] The recent formation of DHS from elements of many independent agencies represented a very large-scale example of such a reorganization and is broadly viewed to have involved substantial transition costs. Transition costs in creating a new agency would be associated with the disruption caused by moving around organizations in the current intelligence system and attempting to forge them into a single agency. The costs could be financial, but interviewees for the study emphasized that costs could also arise because of disruption in the performance of current efforts to prevent terrorist attacks. One transition cost might thus be an increased risk of terrorism in the short term.

---

6 See, for example, the experience of the FBI and its Virtual Case File systems modernization (Eggen and Witte, 2006).

7 For example, interviewees during the study were split as to whether they thought public concern about privacy and civil liberties would make it difficult or even impossible to create a new domestic intelligence agency.

Other possible intangible costs include the potential effects of the new agency and its activities on personal privacy and on civil liberties.[8]

Whether there would be such costs is an open question. On one hand, separating intelligence collection from law enforcement—that is, from the ability to act on that intelligence—could make a new service more acceptable to the public. On the other, there could be concerns over the effects of consolidating activities and information currently located in separate agencies, and the activities and practices of a new agency might raise concerns.

Assessing the size of potential privacy and civil liberties effects or assigning a "monetary value" to such costs for the purposes of this type of an analysis is both controversial and difficult. The central way that values are assigned to such intangibles is trying to determine how much individuals would be willing to pay to avoid the reduction in privacy[9]—that is, how much citizens would be willing to pay to *not* be included in government databases like the various lists that trigger additional screening or bar individuals from traveling (U.S. Government Accountability Office, 2006). When individuals file lawsuits regarding perceived civil liberties infringements, the amounts of judgments can be used to assign values to different negative effects of counterterrorism activities.

In the end, it is a matter of values, and others would undoubtedly assign higher values for the potential intangible costs associated with creating a new domestic intelligence agency, we chose to use a low value for these costs, $1 per person per year, in the assessment. While this number might seem unreasonably low, because it is estimated on a per-person basis, the total cost associated with it still adds up: Since the

---

[8] There are broader civil liberties concerns associated with domestic intelligence activities that, though not necessarily linked to the organizational structure of the domestic intelligence enterprise, could be affected by the decision to create a new domestic agency. For example, one concern is whether domestic intelligence collection produces a "chilling effect" on individuals' willingness to exercise their freedom of expression, dissent, or assembly or to take advantage of government services (see, for example, Solove, 2006, and Taipale, 2004–2005).

[9] For example, studies have been done making estimates of individuals' willingness to pay money to conceal specific pieces of information about themselves producing varied results.

population of the United States is approximately 300 million people, even an average cost of $1 each adds up to $300 million annually.

It should be noted that assigning a privacy and civil liberties *cost* accepts the assumption that a new domestic intelligence agency would be more intrusive or increase the chances of civil liberties curtailment above those imposed by the current arrangements of agencies and organizations involved in domestic intelligence. While this is a reasonable assumption, the opposite is also possible. If a new agency were viewed as better able to protect privacy and civil liberties than the current domestic intelligence enterprise, these potential *costs* would instead be *benefits* that could partly offset the creation or transition costs of a new agency.

Considering Benefits

The level of terrorism risk to the country and how effective the agency would be in mitigating that risk will drive the benefits of creating a new agency. In previous work examining the costs and benefits of regulations intended to reduce the risk of terrorism, RAND has used the results of probabilistic risk modeling to make estimates of expected losses from terrorism on an annual basis. These estimates rely on models created for the insurance industry and use physical modeling of different attack types to estimate dollar costs associated with physical damages, injuries and fatalities, and some types of business interruption. Using this model and additional analysis using higher values for dollar costs associated with injuries and fatalities, one study produced an estimate of expected annualized terrorism losses between $1 billion and $10 billion (LaTourrette and Willis, 2007). This is not to say that this level of losses would be expected *every* year, but that over longer periods the *average* yearly losses would fall in this range.

Because these models do not take into account the full range of costs associated with terrorism (for example, other costs caused by fear of potential terrorist attack),[10] we chose to use a broader range of average annual losses, from $100 million to $100 billion. For comparison, estimates of the total cost of the September 11 terrorist attacks have

[10] See Jackson, Dixon, and Greenfield (2007) for a review.

ranged between $50 billion to over $100 billion dollars,[11] putting the overall average annual losses for 2001 to 2006 from approximately $8 billion to above $17 billion. As a result, estimated annual loss figures at the low end of our range would correspond to a reduced level of risk from that baseline, while supporting terrorist risk values at the upper end of our range ($100 billion annually) would require either repeated attacks at the scale of September 11 or rarer but much larger incidents (e.g., nuclear detonations in cities) that could produce much higher damage levels.

For a given expected level of annual loses, the maximum counterterrorism *benefit* of a particular intelligence effort would be to reduce terrorism risk by 100 percent and reduce the expected loss to zero. This corresponds, for our range of terrorism losses, to a potential benefit range from $100 million to $100 billion per year, depending on the assumed level of terrorist risk the country faces. We used these values to calculate "how effective an agency would need to be" for its benefits to justify its costs: For example, at an expected annual loss level of $100 million, an agency that cost $100 million per year would have to eliminate the risk of terrorist attack completely in order to break even. On the other hand, at an expected annual loss rate of $10 billion dollars, an agency that cost $100 million per year would only have to reduce terrorism risk by 1 percent to break even.[12]

---

[11] Natural Hazards Research and Applications Information Center, University of Colorado (2001); U.S. General Accounting Office (2002b).

[12] While the primary focus of this analysis is intelligence focused on the threat of terrorism, capabilities put in place in response to the terrorist threat could have other associated benefits. Activities related to domestic counterterrorism analysis could also contribute to traditional law enforcement and intelligence-led policing, national counter-drug and counter-money-laundering efforts, other protective or risk-management missions, or could provide other benefits not related to terrorism. There could also be other intangible benefits associated with creation of a new intelligence agency. For example it might address a simple desire to "do something" in response to the terrorist threat and, by doing so, reduce feelings of fear in the general public. Any value ascribed to that reduction would constitute an intangible benefit and, as discussed previously, if that increased safety resulted in fewer behavioral changes that had associated economic costs, could translate to a tangible benefit.

A Qualitative Break-Even Analysis for Creating a New Domestic Intelligence Agency

So, how effective would a new counterterrorism intelligence agency need to be for its benefits to justify the costs of creating it? Figure 6.1 presents a set of break-even curves showing the required performance of a new agency for different cost levels for creating a new agency at different levels of terrorism risk. The break-even effectiveness of a new agency—the "critical risk reduction," or how much it must reduce terrorism risk for its costs to be justified—is shown on the vertical axis for a range of agency costs increasing from $200 million per year up to a high of $1 billion per year.

First, what this analysis shows most clearly is that the choice to create a new agency turns in large part on the assumed level of terrorism risk faced by the United States, a topic on which experts and

Figure 6.1
Critical Risk Reduction Levels for Domestic Intelligence Arrangements of Various Annual Costs at Different Levels of Annual Terrorism Risk

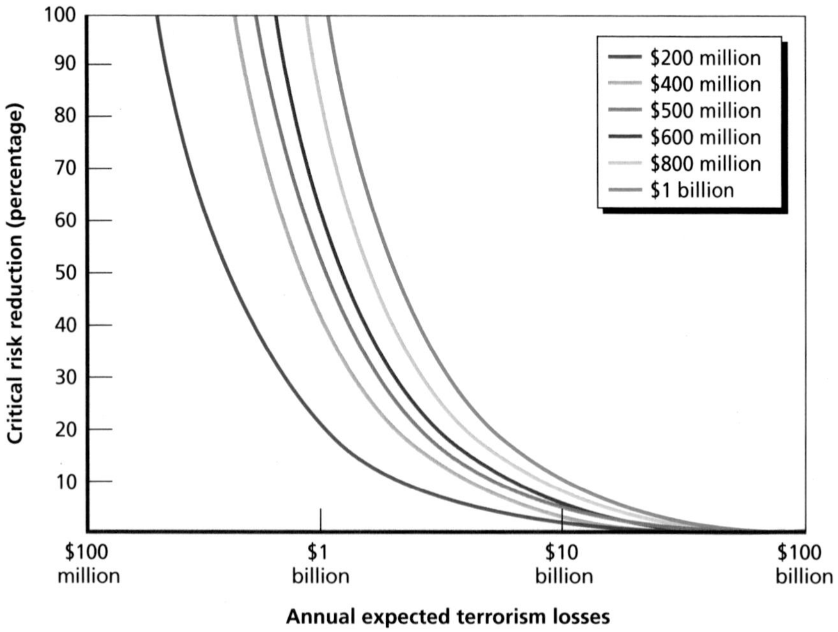

RAND *MG767-6.1*

policymakers differ widely. Looking at the middle range of terrorism risk values (e.g., from $1 billion to $10 billion annual losses), in most cases a new organization would have to be quite effective to justify its costs when the risk is relatively low, and it could be less effective and still justify its performance when the risk is high. As Figure 6.1 shows, for example, looking at the line for a $1 billion agency, and assuming the annual risk of terrorism is $10 billion, the agency justifies its costs—breaks even—if it reduces the annual risk of terrorism risk by only 10 percent.

Lower cost models require lower levels of risk reduction, though if the terrorism risk is closer to the $1 billion per year level, even less expensive models of a new agency must be very effective to be justified. If models were implemented whose costs were greater than our $1 billion upper estimate, the bar for their performance would be even higher. On the other hand, if the assumed annual losses from terrorism are thought to be very high, approaching the $100 billion per year level, even a modestly effective agency can be justified at relatively high absolute cost.[13]

So, which is the "right" curve to use? Cost estimates for a hypothetical new agency must necessarily be speculative, but an example of how a cost value might be chosen is as follows: Based on estimates for the transition costs associated with the creation of the Department of Homeland Security prepared by the Congressional Budget Office, an annual cost of $200 million associated with the reorganization and other costs involved in forming a new agency could be a starting point. Although the privacy and civil liberties effects of creating a new domestic intelligence agency are not entirely clear, it is highly likely that at least part of the population would view its creation as negative in these respects. As a result, for the purposes of illustration, if a value of $1 per American citizen per year is chosen to represent these intangible costs, this would correspond to an additional annual cost of $300 million per year. At these cost levels, the "right" curve would correspond to a total

---

13 While perceptions about the risk of terrorism at that level differ, it may also be the case that more cost-effective means could be found to address those threats than creating a new intelligence organization.

cost of $500 million annually, falling in the center of the range shown in Figure 6.1. At this level, the break-even requirement would vary, for example, from 50 percent risk reduction at the $1 billion level of terrorism risk to 5 percent at the $10 billion risk level.

However, reasonable people will differ about the scope of the costs and benefits of creating a new agency. Some may think that an agency will cost more to put in place than the estimate of $200 million per year. Indeed, DHS's creation did not go as smoothly as some expected, so the Congressional Budget Office's *a priori* cost estimates referenced here may not fully reflect the actual costs of its formation. Views of the privacy and civil liberties costs will almost certainly differ and could shape the outcome of the analysis significantly. For instance, even a modest increase in the average perceived cost per person to $2 per year would add another $300 million dollars to the bill for a new agency, while designing a new agency in a way that protected privacy and civil liberties better than current arrangements would eliminate this cost or even turn it into a benefit.[14]

In the interest of simplifying this discussion, this analysis also leaves out a variety of intangible and other transition costs. For example, concern about whether intelligence will chill individuals' exercise of their rights and participation in political debate and dissent is real, but we did not attempt to include a value for such a chilling effect. There may be other costs that should be included as well, such as how creating a new agency might affect on the perceptions of the United States abroad. For example, there have been concerns that other U.S. domestic security policies have reduced international travel to this

[14] A significant body of literature deals with ways that intelligence activities can be carried out and overseen in an effort to preserve privacy and reduce potential effects on civil liberties. For example, all of the countries examined in this study appear to have specialized oversight structures for controlling the use of broad intelligence-gathering powers. Similarly, application of information technology security, anonymization, auditing, and good information practices also provide ways to carry out intelligence activities while limiting their effects on the general population. See, for example, Teufel (2007); National Research Council, Committee on the Role of Information Technology in Responding to Terrorism (2003); Markle Foundation Task Force (2002, pp. 76–78), Lavin (1982), DHS and U.S. Department of Justice (no date); Dempsey and Flint (2004), and Taipale (2005).

country, producing significant economic costs.[15] If there are transition costs associated with disruption of current activities during the period of reorganization, those would increase the costs as well, though only in the short term as the disruption was resolved.

Approaches such as break-even analysis, though imperfect, enable participants in policy debate to weigh different factors in a common way—rather than, for example, simply debating the potential tradeoff between security and privacy in the abstract. As a result, such an approach can provide a framework for debate even if it cannot necessarily provide a precise answer to the question of whether a new domestic counterterrorism intelligence agency should be created.

If policymakers or other individuals disagree about the advisability of creating a new domestic intelligence agency, such a common framework provides a systematic way to identify *why* they disagree, along with a blueprint for further study to bound the debate. Is it because they differ on what they believe the terrorist threat is, or do they diverge on the likely effectiveness of a reorganized domestic intelligence effort? Disagreements over such factors would not be surprising, nor would identifying the source of the disagreement necessarily lead to consensus and agreement. Still, a policy debate that recognizes and addresses the sources of difference has the potential to be more productive than simply a fight over different final conclusions.

---

[15] See survey results and discussion of travel volume and balance numbers presented at Meserve and Ahlers (2007) and Travel Industry Association of America (2007).

CHAPTER SEVEN

Conclusions: The Path Forward

Caution and deliberations are the watchwords of this study's conclusions. Data for judging performance are in short supply, uncertainties are large, and many of the critical issues turn on values. What we have suggested is a framework for sharpening and enriching the debate. Here, we identify information that would advance the discussion of a major policy issue within that framework.

Beyond broad concerns about the current system, there is little information to actually *assess* its performance, nor to argue persuasively that the performance of a reorganized system would be clearly better than the status quo. How a new domestic intelligence agency would function within the already complex domestic intelligence environment is also not clear and would depend on how much and what parts of the current system were combined to create it. If the new agency were only one of many federal level intelligence agencies, the same complexities inherent in the current intelligence community would afflict it as well. Invariably, any new agency would still have to work across organizational boundaries to interact with law enforcement and other organizations at the state and local level. In an area where direct assessment and analysis are limited, there is a need to consider carefully the implications and potential outcomes of significant policy changes, such as the creation of new organizations or the reorganization for ongoing efforts across a web of institutions and people at many levels inside and outside government.

One argument supporting the contention that the United States needs such an agency is that a number of fellow democracies have them. The examination of a half dozen of those nations identified strengths of those arrangements, along with some enduring problems, but their experience does not make a compelling argument for policy change. Countries with domestic intelligence agencies have not been immune from terrorist attack, including attacks since the September 11 attacks on the United States. It is easy to note differences in the way other democracies have organized domestic security efforts, but it is not immediately obvious that *different* necessarily means *better*.[1] Indeed, some international trends are going in the opposite direction, toward merging law enforcement and intelligence—for instance, the merger of RG and DST in France, or new regional task forces in Britain combining MI5 and the Metropolitan Police.

This is not to say that there are not important concerns with current efforts—both regarding their capability to prevent terrorist attack and the acceptability of their effects on the American public. However, many actions could be taken in response, and major reorganization is only one of them. Indeed, though changes in organizational structure would have an effect on some of the concerns that have been raised, their solutions will most likely not come from structural change alone. Their solutions are as much about what a new agency would be tasked to do and what controls would be placed on its activities as about where in an organizational chart it would fall.

Because the values at play are so fundamental—from concern for life and liberty to fundamental trust in government—designing capable intelligence efforts that are also acceptable to the American people is a delicate balancing act. There is no "right" balance among the many factors that intelligence affect and, even if there were, differences among individual citizens' preferences would mean that right balance would differ from person to person. Any balance will also be unstable over time: The costs that society is willing to pay will be driven in part by how grave the threat is from terrorism. The threat will change, and, even

[1] For example, "Even if we assume that the Brits' MI5 is 'better' than our FBI at fighting terrorism, that may have little to do with its structure and much more to do with its methods of training, its long history of fighting a domestic terrorist threat, and the personnel it has attracted to an agency long been devoted to doing just that" (Juliette Kayyem, quoted in Posner and Kayyem, 2006).

at a single point in time, judgments about its magnitude can both differ greatly across citizens and be volatile in response to events across the body politic. Major events, such as the September 11 attacks, can cause seismic readjustments in public perceptions of threat and risk, leading to demands for major expansion in security and intelligence activities that can overwhelm other concerns—at least in the short term.

At the same time, the public also finds it difficult to assess what intelligence organizations actually do. As a result, allegations of ineffectiveness or inappropriate behavior may lead to concerns that rival the concern about the threat those organizations are meant to address. Transparency and public investigation when problems are discovered can impose accountability and rebuild public trust in institutions after inappropriate behavior comes to light.

Given the necessity for secrecy in intelligence, though, full transparency is generally not feasible. As a result, when problems do arise, the public may have no easy way to judge whether they should be viewed as isolated instances of overstepping or are instead indications of more widespread abuse. How the creation of a new domestic intelligence agency would play out on the court of public opinion is similarly unclear. Most public opinion surveys on the topic lack the specificity to provide much insight into likely future events, and experts and practitioners differ markedly. Even among the practitioners interviewed for this study, views covered a wide range on whether the response to creating a new agency would be strongly positive, negative, or somewhere in between.

These strong pressures on both sides of the issue make domestic intelligence a particularly difficult policy area. The political process can be pressed in one direction or another by events such as a major attack, on the one hand, or disclosures about overzealous intelligence efforts on the other. Overreaction is almost inevitable. Individuals with differing perspectives on both the threat and intelligence efforts to combat it have characterized actions taken since September 11 as overshooting in both directions, either overreacting toward tightening security[2] or hampering the activities of intelligence organizations.[3] These pressures underscore the importance of building reasonable ways for public debate on intelligence issues, choices, and the tradeoffs they involve—and to design domestic intelligence efforts that can adjust as the pressures change in either direction. The idea would be to reduce the chance of dramatic changes that overshoot either by expanding intelligence powers beyond the point where they are acceptable to the public or restricting them so tightly that the price in reduced security becomes too high.

So, if the central conclusion of this effort is that insufficient information is available to make a clear policy choice, then what information should be developed to inform future choices? Our work suggests there are three central requirements:

1. *Build the Needed Foundation.* Before considering alternative organizational models for domestic intelligence, clear policy must be made about what the nation expects its domestic intelligence efforts to do and not do. Broad goals such as preventing terrorism, as we have seen, are not enough to link what is being done to the outcomes it is intended to achieve. David Heyman (2000) has referred to this as the need for a "framework" for domestic intelligence: articulating what exactly we want domestic intelligence efforts to do, what is permissible for government to do in the process, and how activities must be overseen to ensure that actual efforts are within permissible boundaries. These are all choices that define what domestic intelligence is intended to achieve, and these choices must precede discussions

2 For example, passage of the USA PATRIOT Act in the weeks after September 11 broadly expanding domestic intelligence powers.

3 For example, the wholesale cancellation of some intelligence programs—such as the DHS TIPS Program or the Defense Advanced Research Project Agency's (DARPA's) Total (later, Terrorism) Information Awareness program.

of organizational change. Without them, attempts to weigh the value of reorganization largely lack the scales needed to do so.

2. *Better Understand the System We Have.* In discussing the current domestic intelligence enterprise, we described the complexity of the current system. Agencies at all levels of government and even in the private sector have roles in domestic intelligence activities. Information systems and coordinating entities such as federal task forces, JTTFs, and fusion centers link many organizations together in web-like ways. Different agencies collect intelligence information in different ways, for different purposes.

While it is clear that the network of organizations that make up the domestic intelligence enterprise is complex, the full implications of that complexity are not clear. How much duplication is there actually in collection and analysis? Which information-sharing channels are important versus which are simply formal links with little actual relevance to current activities? Is the system really as complex as it appears? Without understanding the actual activities of the varied organizations, it is difficult to estimate the benefit of simplifying the system through reorganization and condensation of activities into a new domestic intelligence agency.

3. *Collect Actual Data on the Performance of the Current Domestic Intelligence Enterprise.* Predicting the costs of a new domestic intelligence agency is difficult, but their general magnitude is discernible. That is less so for benefits. For instance, data are available about neither the performance of current intelligence activities nor the likely performance of a reorganized system. Responding to that absence, we framed our discussion in the language of break-even analysis and left it to the readers to assess individually how much creating a new agency might reduce the risk of terrorist attack.

How might such information be developed to support future deliberations in this area? Yes, some of the desirable data are unknowable, such as the number of clandestine terrorist cells present in the country at any given time. But other relevant information could certainly be collected:

- Looking at the functioning of the current system, when and why have the plots that have been detected been observed? Are the ways they have been detected suggestive of systematic success (i.e., they have been caught in ways that are likely to capture other plots as well), or were they the result of lucky circumstances? Though some relevant events are publicly known, a full understanding of current performance will necessarily require a broader picture of organizational activities than is available in the public domain.
- What is the "false alarm" rate, and what have been the implications of mistakenly flagging individuals or behaviors as threatening? Though some high-profile cases and suggestive data about the yield of domestic intelligence activities are available publicly, it is not clear how complete this information is, nor how representative it is of the functioning of the system overall.
- Are there "natural experiments" that could provide information on how the system performed in other contexts that could gauge its likely performance for terrorism? For example, are there other events where information reported at the state or local level detected in one part of the country needed to travel up to the federal level and outward to other organizations rapidly enough to be acted on? Cases associated with traditional law enforcement, public health, or other government areas of responsibility could provide such cases for indirect assessment of all or part of the system's performance.

Such data collection and assessment would clearly face security concerns, just as ongoing oversight and assessment of counterterrorism efforts necessarily require access to sensitive information. The collection and assessment would similarly require openness on the part of individual agencies to a level of self-examination and could impinge on individual organizational equities in the process. However, particularly with the creation of the position of Director of National Intelligence and its mission to bring together national intelligence efforts, such problems are, in principle, solvable. Without doing so, the lack of basic information on the scope of the problems with current efforts will persist, and it will remain impossible to say whether reorganization—or one of the many other approaches to improve organizational performance—is in the nation's interest. Further, a level of transparency is needed to make the argument either for change or for maintaining the status quo, and to achieve public support for a decision to take—or not take—action to reorganize domestic intelligence activities.

Whatever the reasons why the United States has not had a major terrorist attack in the six years since September 11, 2001, the threat of international and domestic terrorism has not disappeared, nor is it likely ever to do so entirely. Political violence has been an element of the strategies of nonstate groups throughout human history, so developing appropriate responses to defend against attacks will remain an important national concern. Major questions in that process are (1) How should domestic intelligence efforts be structured? and (2) What are the implications of how domestic intelligence efforts are organized, in terms of both their capability and, particularly in the American context, their acceptability to the public they are intended to protect? While many of the questions defy easy answers, continuing to ask them—and developing ways to weigh the full range of critical, and sometimes competing, concerns with intelligence policies—remains an important part of the national debate.

APPENDIX A

Expert Panel Participants

Marion Bowman
John Brennan
Joan Dempsey
Michael German
Richard Jerome
Richard Posner
Suzanne Spaulding
John P. Sullivan
John Yoo

APPENDIX B

Domestic Program Map

The RAND team's mapping of the current U.S. domestic intelligence enterprise is presented in Figure B.1. However, the size of the U.S. domestic intelligence enterprise makes the resulting map of it ill-suited for presentation in a book format. Readers are encouraged to view the larger version of this image available at

http://www.rand.org/pubs/monographs/MG767/

Figure B.1
The U.S. Domestic Intelligence Enterprise

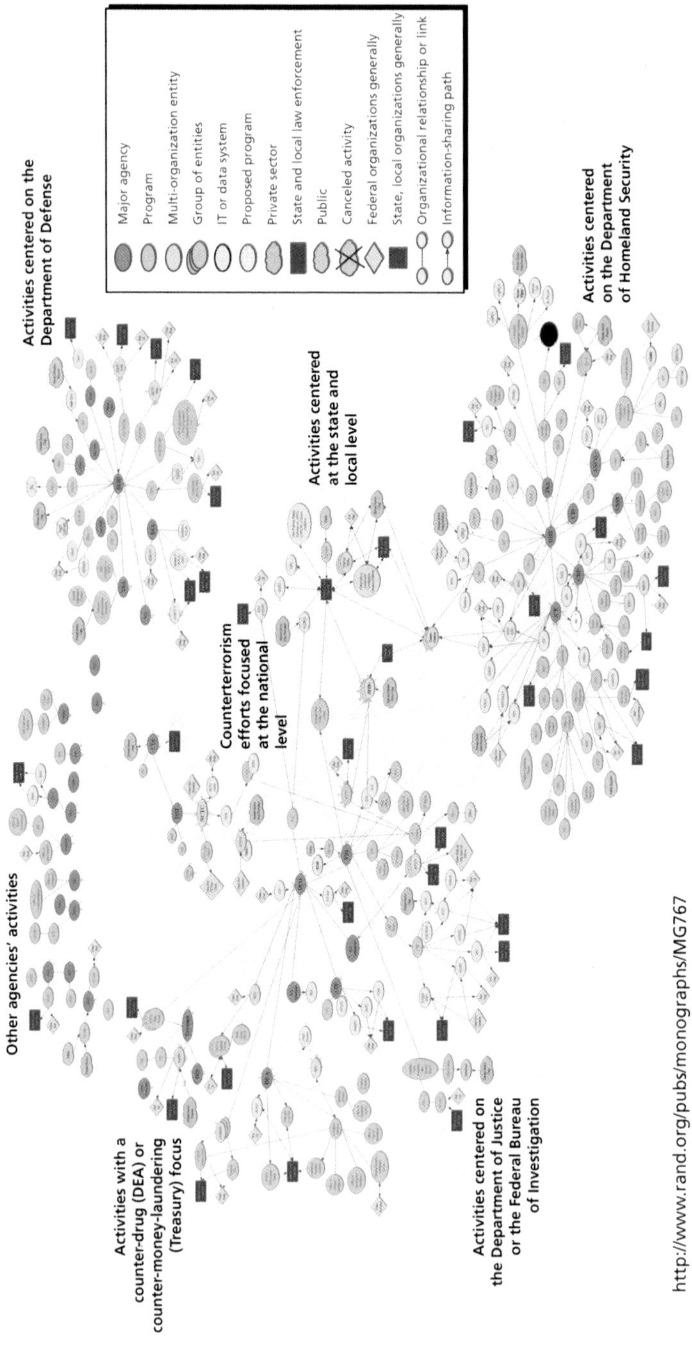

http://www.rand.org/pubs/monographs/MG767

References

9/11 Commission—*see* National Commission on Terrorist Attacks on the United States.

"Australia to Double Spy Personnel," *BBC News*, October 17, 2005.

Advisory Panel to Assess Domestic Response Capabilities for Terrorism Involving Weapons of Mass Destruction (the "Gilmore Commission"), "IV. Implementing the National Strategy," December 15, 2002.

American Civil Liberties Union, *No Real Threat: The Pentagon's Secret Database on Peaceful Protest*, New York, January 2007.

American Enterprise Institute for Public Policy Research, *Public Opinion on the War with Iraq*, Washington, D.C., March 14, 2008. As of May 14, 2008:
http://www.aei.org/publications/pubID.22142/pub_detail.asp

———, *America and the War on Terror*, Washington, D.C., November 29, 2007. As of May 14, 2008:
http://www.aei.org/publications/pubID.22819/pub_detail.asp

Andrews, Edmund, L., "Threats and Responses: Liberty and Security: New Scale for Toting Up Lost Freedom vs. Security Would Measure in Dollars," *New York Times*, March 11, 2003, p. 13.

Australian Security Intelligence Organisation, *Annual Report to Parliament 2004–2005*, Canberra, 2005.

———, *Annual Report to Parliament 2005–2006*, Canberra, 2006.

Austen, Ian, "In Break from History and Scandal, Canada Chooses a Civilian to Lead the Mounties," *New York Times*, July 7, 2007a.

———, "Deported Canadian Was No Threat, Report Says," *New York Times*, August 10, 2007b.

Berman, Jerry, and Laura Flint, "Guiding Lights: Intelligence Oversight and Control for the Challenge of Terrorism," *Criminal Justice Ethics*, Winter/Spring 2003, pp. 2, 56–58.

Best, Samuel J., and Monika L. McDermott, "Measuring Opinions vs. Non-Opinions—The Case of the USA Patriot Act," *The Forum*, Vol. 5, No. 2, 2007.

Birrer, Frans A. J., "Data Mining to Combat Terrorism and the Roots of Privacy Concerns," *Ethics and Information Technology*, Vol. 7, 2005, pp. 211–220.

Block, Robert, "FBI Alters Tactics in Fight Against Terrorists," *Wall Street Journal*, May 23, 2007, p. B1.

Brown, Gordon, "Securing Our Future," speech at the Royal United Services Institute, London, UK, February 13, 2006. As of May 23, 2008: http://www.hm-treasury.gov.uk/newsroom_and_speeches/speeches/chancellorexchequer/speech_chex_130206.cfm

Burch, James, "A Domestic Intelligence Agency for the United States? A Comparative Analysis of Domestic Intelligence Agencies and Their Implications for Homeland Security," *Homeland Security Affairs*, Vol. III, No. 2, June 2007.

Bureau of Justice Assistance, U.S. Department of Justice, *Intelligence-Led Policing: The New Intelligence Architecture*, Washington, D.C., NCJ 210681, September 2005.

Business Executives for National Security, "Recommendations for Improving the Suspicious Activity Report (SAR)," April 11, 2003.

Byman, Daniel, "US Counter-Terrorism Options: A Taxonomy," *Survival*, Vol. 49, No. 3, 2007, pp. 121–150.

"Canadian Agencies Were Warned of Air India in Attack," *CBC News*, April 30, 2007.

Canadian Society for Industrial Security, "Accountability and Review," *Backgrounder Series*, No. 2, Ottawa, November 2004, p. 2.

———, "The CSIS Mandate," *Backgrounder Series*, No. 1, Ottawa, February 2005, p. 1.

Carter, Ashton, John Deutch, and Philip Zelikow, "Catastrophic Terrorism: Tackling the New Danger," *Foreign Affairs*, November–December 1998.

Carter, Josh, "Transcending the Nuclear Framework: Deterrence and Compellence as Counter-Terrorism Strategies," *Low Intensity Conflict and Law Enforcement*, Vol. 10, No. 2, Summer 2001, pp. 84–102.

Chesney, Robert M., "Civil Liberties and the Terrorism Prevention Paradigm: The Guilt By Association Critique," *Michigan Law Review*, Vol. 101, No. 6, May 2003, pp. 1408–1452.

Clarke, Richard A., and Rand Beers, *The Forgotten Homeland: A Century Foundation Task Force Report*, New York, NY: The Century Foundation Press, 2006.

Commission of Inquiry into the Actions of Canadian Officials in Relation to Maher Arar, *Report of the Events Relating to Maher Arar: Analysis and Recommendations*, Ottawa: Public Works and Government Services Canada, 2006.

Commission on the Intelligence Capabilities of the United States Regarding Weapons of Mass Destruction, *Report to the President of the United States*, March 31, 2005.

Congressional Budget Office, *Cost Estimate: H.R. 5005, Homeland Security Act of 2002*, Washington, D.C., July 9, 2002.

Crumpton, Henry A., "Intelligence and Homeland Defense," Chapter 12 in Jennifer E. Sims and Burton Gerber, eds., *Transforming U.S. Intelligence*, Washington, D.C.: Georgetown University Press, 2005.

Daft, Richard L., *Organization Theory and Design*, Mason, Ohio: Thomson/South Western, 2004.

Davis, Ann, "Why a 'No Fly List' Aimed at Terrorists Delays Others," *Wall Street Journal*, April 22, 2003, p. 1.

Davis, Paul K., and Brian Michael Jenkins, *Deterrence and Influence in Counterterrorism: A Component in the War on al Qaeda*, Santa Monica, Calif.: RAND Corporation, MR-1619-DARPA, 2002. As of May 14, 2008:
http://www.rand.org/pubs/monograph_reports/MR1619/

Davis, Darren W., and Brian D. Silver, "Civil Liberties vs. Security: Public Opinion in the Context of the Terrorist Attacks on America," *American Journal of Political Science*, Vol. 48, No. 1, January 2004, pp. 28–46.

Dempsey, James X., and Lara M. Flint, "Commercial Data and National Security," *The George Washington Law Review*, Vol. 72, No. 6, August 2004.

Denning, Lord, *The Denning Report: The Profumo Affair*, London, HMSO 1963, Pimlico reprint, 1992.

Department of the Prime Minister and Cabinet (Australia), *Protecting Australia Against Terrorism 2006*, Canberra, 2006.

DeRosa, Mary, "Data Mining and Data Analysis for Counterterrorism," Center for Strategic and International Studies, March 2004.

Deutch, John, "Strengthening U.S. Intelligence," Statement to the National Commission on Terrorist Attacks Upon the United States, October 14, 2003. As of May 13, 2008:
http://www.9-11commission.gov/hearings/hearing4/witness_deutch.htm

DeYoung, Karen, "A Fight Against Terrorism—and Disorganization," *Washington Post*, August 9, 2006, p. A1.

DHS—*see* U.S. Department of Homeland Security.

"Do We Need an MI5?" transcript of *Frontline* interview, Web page, October 16, 2003. As of May 14, 2008:
http://www.pbs.org/wgbh/pages/frontline/shows/sleeper/fbi/mi5.html

DOJ OIG—*see* U.S. Department of Justice, Office of the Inspector General.

Don, Bruce W., David R. Frelinger, Scott Gerwehr, Eric Landree, and Brian A. Jackson, *Network Technologies for Networked Terrorists: Assessing the Value of Information and Communication Technologies to Modern Terrorist Organizations*, Santa Monica, Calif.: RAND Corporation, TR-454-DHS, 2007. As of May 13, 2008:
http://www.rand.org/pubs/technical_reports/TR454/

Eggen, Dan, "Lawsuits May Illuminate Methods of Spy Program," *Washington Post*, August 14, 2007, p. A1.

Eggen, Dan, and Griff Witte, "The FBI's Upgrade That Wasn't," *Washington Post*, August 18, 2006, p. A1.

Eisenhardt, Kathleen M., "Making Fast Decisions in High-Velocity Environments," *Academy of Management Journal*, Vol. 32, 1989, pp. 543–576.

English, Larry P., "Information Quality: Critical Ingredient for National Security," *Journal of Database Management*, Vol. 16, No. 1, January–March 2005, pp. 18–32.

European Commission for Democracy Through Law (Venice Commission), *Report on the Democratic Oversight of the Security Services*, June 11, 2007. As of May 14, 2008:
http://www.venice.coe.int/docs/2007/CDL-AD(2007)016-e.asp

Fay, Stephen J., "Tough on Crime, Tough on Civil Liberties: Some Negative Aspects of Britain's Wholesale Adoption of CCTV Surveillance During the 1990s," *International Review of Law, Computers and Technology*, Vol. 12, No. 2, July 1998, pp. 315–347.

Federal Bureau of Investigation, *FY 2008 Authorization and Budget Request to Congress*, 2007.

"Feds Sharpen Secret Tools for Data Mining," *USA Today*, July 20, 2006.

Final Report of the Select Committee to Study Governmental Operations with Respect to Intelligence Activities of the United States Senate, 94th Congress, 2nd Session, 1976, Book II, *Intelligence Activities and the Rights of Americans*, and Book III, *Supplementary Detailed Staff Reports on Intelligence Activities and the Rights of Americans.*

Fischoff, Baruch, et al., "Judged Terror Risks and Proximity to the World Trade Center," *Journal of Risk and Uncertainty,* Vol. 26, No. 2/3, 2003, pp. 137–151.

Galbraith, Jay R., Designing Complex Organizations, Reading, Mass.: Addison-Wesley, 1973.

———, *Designing Organizations: An Executive Briefing on Strategy, Structure, and Process*, San Francisco, Calif.: Jossey-Bass, 1995.

Gilmore Commission—*see* Advisory Panel to Assess Domestic Response Capabilities for Terrorism Involving Weapons of Mass Destruction.

Halperin, Morton H., "National Security and Civil Liberties," *Foreign Policy*, No. 21, Winter 1975–1976, pp. 125–160.

Hammond, Thomas H., "Why Is the Intelligence Community So Difficult to Redesign? Smart Practices, Conflicting Goals, and the Creation of Purpose-Based Organizations," *Governance: An International Journal of Policy, Administration, and Institutions*, Vol. 20, No. 3, July 2007, pp. 401–422.

Hamre, John J., statement to the National Commission on Terrorist Attacks Upon the United States, December 8, 2003. As of May 14, 2008:
http://www.9-11commission.gov/hearings/hearing6/witness_hamre.htm

Harris, Shane, "TIA Lives On," *National Journal*, February 23, 2006a, p. 66.

——— "Terrorist Profiling, Version 2.0," *National Journal*, October 20, 2006b, p. 57

Herman, Tom, "IRS Combats Its In-House Snoops," *Wall Street Journal*, December 19, 2007, p. D3.

Heyman, David, "Finding the Enemy Within: Towards a Framework for Domestic Intelligence," in Bert B. Tussing, ed., *Threats at Our Threshold: Homeland Defense and Homeland Security in the New Century*, Washington, D.C.: Center for Strategic and International Studies, 2000, pp. 149–174. As of May 13, 2008:
http://www.csis.org/images/stories/HomelandSecurity/071022_Chap4-FindingTheEnemyWithin.pdf

Home Office Communication Directorate (United Kingdom), *Guidelines on Special Branch Work in the United Kingdom*, March 2004.

Hsu, Spencer S., and Robert O'Harrow, Jr., "DHS to Replace 'Duplicative' Anti-Terrorism Data Network," *Washington Post*, January 18, 2008, p. A3.

Huber, George P., and Richard L. Daft, "The Information Environments of Organizations" in Frederic M. Jablin et al., eds., *Handbook of Organizational Communication: An Interdisciplinary Perspective,* Newbury Park, Calif.: Sage, 1987.

Huddy, Leonie, "Threat, Anxiety, and Support of Antiterrorism Policies," *American Journal of Political Science,* Vol. 49, No. 3, July 2005, pp. 593–608.

Jackson, Brian A., Lloyd Dixon, and Victoria A. Greenfield, *Economically Targeted Terrorism: A Review of the Literature and a Framework for Considering Defensive Approaches*, Santa Monica, Calif.: RAND Corporation, TR-476-CTRMP, 2007. As of May 14, 2008:
http://www.rand.org/pubs/technical_reports/TR476/

Jiwa, Salim, *The Death of Air India Flight 182*, London: W. H. Allen and Co., 1987.

Johnston, Rob, *The Culture of Analytic Tradecraft: An Ethnography of the IC*, Washington, D.C.: Center for the Study of Intelligence, Central Intelligence Agency, 2005.

Jonas, Jeff, and Jim Harper, "Effective Counterterrorism and the Limited Role of Predictive Data Mining," CATO Institute *Policy Analysis*, No. 584, December 11, 2006.

Koontz, Linda D., *Homeland Security: Continuing Attention to Privacy Concerns Is Needed as Programs Are Developed*, Washington, D.C.: U.S. Government Accountability Office, GAO-07-630T, March 21, 2007.

Larence, Eileen R., *Homeland Security: Preliminary Information on Federal Actions to Address Challenges Faced by State and Local Information Fusion Centers*, Washington, D.C.: U.S. Government Accountability Office, GAO-07-1241T, September 27, 2007.

LaTourrette, Tom, and Henry H. Willis, "Using Probabilistic Terrorism Risk Modeling for Regulatory Benefit-Cost Analysis: Application to the Western Hemisphere Travel Initiative Implemented in the Land Environment," Santa Monica, Calif.: RAND Corporation, WR-487-IEC, 2007. As of May 14, 2008: http://www.rand.org/pubs/working_papers/WR487/

Lavin, Marvin, *Intelligence Constraints of the 1970s and Domestic Terrorism: Volume II: Survey of Legal, Legislative, and Administrative Constraints*, Santa Monica, Calif.: RAND Corporation, N-1902-DOJ, 1982. As of May 14, 2008: http://www.rand.org/pubs/notes/N1902/

Lahneman, William J., "Knowledge-Sharing in the Intelligence Community After September 11th," *International Journal of Intelligence and Counterintelligence*, Vol. 17, 2004, pp. 614–633.

Lee, Christopher, "Defense Department Personnel System Blocked," *Washington Post*, February 27, 2006.

Lewis, David E., *Presidents and the Politics of Agency Design: Political Insulation in the United States Government Bureaucracy, 1946–1997*, Stanford, Calif.: Stanford University Press, 2003.

Lichtblau, Eric, and James Risen, "Spy Agency Mined Vast Data Trove, Officials Report," *New York Times*, December 24, 2005.

Markle Foundation Task Force, *Protecting America's Freedom in the Information Age*, New York: The Markle Foundation, October 2002.

———, *Creating a Trusted Information Network for Homeland Security*, New York: The Markle Foundation, December 2003.

———, *Mobilizing Information to Prevent Terrorism: Accelerating Development of a Trusted Information Sharing Environment*, New York: The Markle Foundation, July 2006.

Marks, Daniel E., and Ivan Y. Sun, "The Impact of September 11th on Organizational Development Among State and Local Law Enforcement Agencies," *Journal of Contemporary Criminal Justice*, Vol. 23, No. 2, 2007, pp. 159–173.

Martin, Kate, "Domestic Intelligence and Civil Liberties," *SAIS Review*, Vol. 24, No. 1, Winter–Spring 2004, pp. 7–21.

Masse, Todd, *Domestic Intelligence in the United Kingdom: Applicability of the MI-5 Model to the United States*, Washington, D.C.: Congressional Research Service, RL31920, May 19, 2003.

———, *Homeland Security Intelligence: Perceptions, Statutory Definitions, and Approaches*, Washington, D.C.: Congressional Research Service, RL33616, August 18, 2006.

Masse, Todd, Siobhan O'Neil, and John Rollins, *Fusion Centers: Issues and Options for Congress*, Washington, D.C.: Congressional Research Service, RL34070, July 6, 2007.

Meserve, Jeanne, and Mike M. Ahlers, "Travel Industry: U.S. Losing Out on International Tourism," CNN.com, January 31, 2007. As of May 14, 2008: http://www.cnn.com/2007/TRAVEL/01/31/international.travel/index.html

Meyer, Alan D., "Adapting to Environmental Jolts," *Administrative Science Quarterly*, Vol. 27, No. 4, December 1982, pp. 515–537.

Moe, Terry, "The Politics of Bureaucratic Structure," in John E. Chubb and Paul E. Peterson, eds., *Can the Government Govern?* Washington, D.C.: The Brookings Institution, 1989.

Milligan, Darric, et al., *Intelligence-Led Policing Tool: Intelligence-Led Policing Technology for State and Local Law Enforcement Agencies*, Bedford, Mass.: Mitretek Corporation, MTR-2006-016, 2006.

Morgan, Richard E., *Domestic Intelligence: Monitoring Dissent in America*, Austin, Tex.: University of Texas, 1980.

Moss, Michael, and Jenny Nordberg, "A Nation At War, Muslims: Imams Urged to Be Alert for Suspicious Visitors," *New York Times*, April 6, 2003.

Nakashima, Ellen, "Customs Breaks Privacy Laws in Data Collection, GAO Says," *Washington Post*, May 16, 2007, p. A2.

National Commission on the Public Service, *Urgent Business for America: Revitalizing the Federal Government for the 21st Century*, January 2003. As of May 23, 2008:
http://www.uscourts.gov/newsroom/VolckerRpt.pdf

National Commission on Terrorist Attacks Upon the United States, *Law Enforcement, Counterterrorism, and Intelligence Collection in the United States Prior to 9/11*, Staff Statement No. 9, Washington, D.C., April 13–14, 2004a.

———, *Threats and Responses in 2001*, Staff Statement No. 10, Washington, D.C., April 13–14, 2004b.

———, *The 9/11 Commission Report*, Washington, D.C., July 22, 2004c.

National Counterterrorism Center, "About the National Counterterrorism Center," Web page, no date. As of May 14, 2008:
http://www.nctc.gov/about_us/about_nctc.html

Natural Hazards Research and Applications Information Center, University of Colorado, *The Terrorist Attacks on September 11, 2001: Immediate Impacts and Their Ramifications for Federal Emergency Management*, Boulder, Co., Quick Response Report #140, 2001. As of May 14, 2008:
http://www.colorado.edu/hazards/research/qr/qr140/qr140.html

National Intelligence Council, *The Terrorist Threat to the U.S. Homeland*, National Intelligence Estimate, Washington, D.C., July 2007.

National Research Council, *Discouraging Terrorism: Some Implications of September 11th*, Washington, D.C.: National Academies Press, 2002.

National Research Council, Committee on the Role of Information Technology in Responding to Terrorism, *Information Technology for Counterterrorism: Immediate Actions and Future Possibilities*, Washington, D.C.: National Academies Press, 2003.

National Response Center, "NCR Background," Web page, no date. As of May 14, 2008:
http://www.nrc.uscg.mil/nrcback.html

National Security Agency, "Frequently Asked Questions: Signals Intelligence," Web page, no date. As of May 14, 2008:
http://www.nsa.gov/about/about00020.cfm

Nye, Joseph S., Jr., "Peering into the Future," *Foreign Affairs*, Vol. 77, No. 4, July/August 1994, pp. 82–93.

"Official: Radicals Wanted to Create Carnage at Fort Dix," CNN.com, May 9, 2007. As of May 14, 2008:
http://www.cnn.com/2007/US/05/08/fortdix.plot/index.html

Orton, James D., "Enactment, Sensemaking, and Decision-Making in the 1976 Reorganization of U.S. Intelligence," *Journal of Management Studies*, Vol. 37, No. 2, March 2000, pp. 213–234.

Perrow, Charles, *Normal Accidents: Living with High-Risk Technologies,* New York: Basic Books, 1984.

Pillar, Paul, "Intelligence," in Audrey Kurth Cronin and James M. Ludes, eds., *Attacking Terrorism: Elements of a Grand Strategy*, Washington, D.C.: Georgetown University Press, 2004.

Pincus, Walter, "Corralling Domestic Intelligence: Standards in the Works for Reports of Suspicious Activity," *Washington Post*, January 13, 2006, p. A5.

Poe, Robert, "The Ultimate Net Monitoring Tool," *Wired*, May 17, 2006.

"Police Had Hint 11 Days Before 1985 Air India Bombing," *CBC News*, May 1, 2007.

Porch, Douglas, *The French Secret Services: From the Dreyfus Affair to the Gulf War*, Oxford, UK: Oxford University Press, 1997.

Porter, Michael, *Competitive Advantage*, New York: Free Press, 1985.

Posner, Richard A., *Uncertain Shield: The U.S. Intelligence System in the Throes of Reform*, Lanham, Md.: Rowman and Littlefield, 2006.

Posner, Richard A., and Juliette Kayyem, "Does the United States Need a New Domestic Intelligence Agency?" Council on Foreign Relations Online Debate, November 13–17, 2006. As of May 15, 2008:
http://www.cfr.org/publication/11990/does_the_united_states_need_a_domestic_intelligence_agency.html

Program Manager, Information Sharing Environment, *Information Sharing Environment Implementation Plan*, November 2006. As of May 14, 2008:
http://www.ise.gov/docs/reports/ise-impplan-200611.pdf

Program on National Security Reform, "Project on National Security Reform Literature Review," no date. As of August 22, 2008:
http://www.pnsr.org/data/images/organizational_structure_literature_review.pdf

Public Law 235, National Security Act of 1947, July 26, 1947.

Public Law 95-511, Foreign Intelligence Surveillance Act of 1978, October 25, 1978.

Public Law 103-62, Government Performance and Results Act of 1993, August 3, 1993.

Public Law 107-56, Uniting and Strengthening America by Providing Appropriate Tools Required to Intercept and Obstruct Terrorism Act of 2001 (USA PATRIOT Act), October 26, 2001.

Public Law 108-458, Intelligence Reform and Terrorism Prevention Act of 2004, December 17, 2004.

Ratcliffe, Jerry H., "Intelligence-Led Policing and the Problems of Turning Rhetoric into Practice," *Policing and Society*, Vol. 12, No. 1, 2002, pp. 53–66.

Reese, Shawn, *Homeland Security Advisory System: Possible Issues for Congressional Oversight*, Washington, D.C.: Congressional Research Service, RL32023, May 19, 2003.

Reeve, Simon, *One Day in September: A Full Story of the 1972 Munich Olympics Massacre*, London: Faber and Faber, 2005.

Riley, K. Jack, Gregory F. Treverton, Jeremy M. Wilson, and Lois M. Davis, *State and Local Intelligence in the War on Terrorism*, Santa Monica, Calif.: RAND Corporation, MG-394-RC, 2005. As of May 14, 2008: http://www.rand.org/pubs/monographs/MG394/

Rishikof, Harvey, "The Role of the Federal Bureau of Investigation in National Security," in Roger George and Robert Kline, eds., *Intelligence and National Security Strategist: Enduring Issues and Challenges*, New York: Rowan and Littlefield Publishers, 2006.

Schertzing, Phillip Daniel, *'Against All Enemies and Opposers Whatever:' The Michigan State Police Crusade Against the 'Un-Americans,' 1917–1977*, Doctoral Dissertation, Michigan State University, Department of History, 1999.

Schulhofer, Stephen J., *The Enemy Within: Intelligence Gathering, Law Enforcement, and Civil Liberties in the Wake of September 11*, New York, NY: Century Foundation Press, 2002.

Schwarz, Fredrick A. O., Jr., "The Church Committee and a New Era of Intelligence Oversight," *Intelligence and National Security*, Vol. 22, No. 2, April 2007, pp. 270–297.

Security Intelligence Review Committee (Canadian), *SIRC Annual Report 2005–2006: An Operational Review of the Canadian Security Intelligence Service*, Ottowa, 2006.

Seifert, Jeffery W., *Data Mining and Homeland Security: An Overview*, Washington, D.C.: Congressional Research Service, RL31798, June 5, 2007.

Shafritz, Jay M., and Albert C. Hyde, eds., *Classics of Public Administration*, Pacific Grove, Calif.: Brooks/Cole, 1992.

Shane, Scott, "C.I.A. to Release Documents on Decades-Old Misdeeds," *New York Times*, June 22, 2007.

Skrzycki, Cindy, "Writing Rules and Pricing Rights at the OMB," *Washington Post*, September 30, 2003, p. E1.

Solomon, John, "FBI Finds It Frequently Overstepped in Collecting Data," *Washington Post*, June 14, 2007, p. A1.

Solove, Daniel J., "A Taxonomy of Privacy," *University of Pennsylvania Law Review*, Vol. 154, No. 3, 2006, p. 477.

Stevenson, Jonathan, "Terrorism and Deterrence," *Survival*, Vol. 46, No. 4, November 2004, pp. 179–185.

Sunstein, Cass R., "Terrorism and Probability Neglect," *Journal of Risk and Uncertainty*, Vol. 26, No. 2/3, 2003, p. 121.

Taipale, K. A., "Technology, Security and Privacy: The Fear of Frankenstein, the Mythology of Privacy and the Lessons of King Ludd," *International Journal of Communications Law and Policy*, No. 9, Winter 2004–2005, pp. 1–98.

Taylor, Eric, "The Department of Homeland Security May Make Americans Less Safe," in James Torr, ed., *Homeland Security*, San Diego, Calif.: Greenhaven Press, 2004.

Technology and Privacy Advisory Council, U.S. Department of Defense, *Safeguarding Privacy in the Fight Against Terrorism*, March 2004.

Teufel, Hugo, III, Chief Privacy Officer, U.S. Department of Homeland Security, "State and Local Information Sharing," Testimony before the Committee on House Homeland Security Subcommittee on Intelligence, Information Sharing and Terrorism Risk Assessment, March 14, 2007.

Travel Industry Association of America, "Economic Research: Economic Impact of Travel and Tourism," Web page, May 2007. As of May 14, 2008:
http://www.tia.org/researchpubs/economic_research_impact_tourism.html

Treverton, Gregory F., "Estimating Beyond the Cold War," *Defense Intelligence Journal*, Vol. 3, No. 2, Fall 1994.

———, "The State of Federal Management," *Government Executive,* January 2004.

Treverton, Gregory F., and C. Bryan Gabbard, *Assessing the Tradecraft of Intelligence Analysis*, Santa Monica, Calif.: RAND Corporation, TR-293, 2008. As of May 14, 2008:
http://www.rand.org/pubs/technical_reports/TR293/

U.S. Department of Homeland Security, *DHS Intelligence Enterprise Strategic Plan,* Washington, D.C., January 2006.

U.S. Department of Homeland Security, "Activities and Programs," no date. As of May 14, 2008:
http://www.dhs.gov/xinfoshare/programs/

U.S. Department of Homeland Security, Data Privacy and Integrity Advisory Committee, *The Use of Commercial Data*, Washington, D.C., Report No. 2006-03, December 6, 2006.

U.S. Department of Homeland Security, Lessons Learned Information Sharing System, "LLIS Intelligence and Information Sharing Initiative: Homeland Security Intelligence Requirements Process," December 2005.

U.S. Department of Homeland Security, Office of the Inspector General, *Review of the Transportation Security Administration Role in the Use and Dissemination of Airline Passenger Data (Redacted),* OIG-05-12, March 2005.

———, *ADVISE Could Support Intelligence Analysis More Effectively*, Washington, D.C., OIG-07-56, June 2007a.

———, *Survey of DHS Intelligence Collection and Dissemination (Unclassified Summary),* Washington, D.C., OIG-07-49, June 2007b.

U.S. Department of Homeland Security and U.S. Department of Justice, "Fusion Center Guidelines: Developing and Sharing Information and Intelligence in a New Era," no date.

U.S. Department of Justice, Office of the Inspector General, *The Federal Bureau of Investigation's Efforts to Improve the Sharing of Intelligence and Other Information* (redacted and unclassified), Washington, D.C., Audit Report 04-10, December 2003.

———, *The Department of Justice's Terrorism Task Forces*, Washington, D.C., Report Number I-2005-007, June 2005a.

———, *Review of United States Attorneys' Offices' Use of Intelligence Research Specialists*, Washington, D.C., I-2006-003, December 2005b.

———, *A Review of the FBI's Handling of the Brandon Mayfield Case* (redacted and unclassified), Washington, D.C., January 2006.

———, *A Review of the Federal Bureau of Investigation's Use of National Security Letters* (redacted and unclassified), Washington, D.C., March 2007a.

———, *Follow-Up Audit of the Federal Bureau of Investigation's Efforts to Hire, Train, and Retain, Intelligence Analysts*, Washington, D.C., Audit Report 07-30, April 2007b.

U.S. Department of State, Office of the Coordinator for Counterterrorism, "Country Report on Terrorism," Web page, April 28, 2006. As of May 14, 2008: http://www.state.gov/s/ct/rls/crt/2005/65970.htm

U.S. General Accounting Office, *Combating Terrorism: How Five Countries Are Organized to Combat Terrorism*, Washington D.C., GAO/NSIAD-00-85, April 2002a.

———, *Review of Studies of the Economic Impact of the September 11, 2001, Terrorist Attacks at the Word Trade Center*, Washington, D.C., GAO-02-700R, May 29, 2002b.

———, *Data Mining: Federal Efforts Cover a Wide Range of Uses*, Washington, D.C., GAO-04-548, May 2004.

U.S. Government Accountability Office, *Maritime Security: New Structures Have Improved Information Sharing, But Security Clearance Processing Requires Further Attention*, Washington, D.C., GAO-05-394, April 2005.

———, *Terrorist Watch List Screening: Efforts to Help Reduce Adverse Effects on the Public*, Washington, D.C., GAO-06-1031, September 2006.

———, *Information Technology: Numerous Federal Networks Used to Support Homeland Security Need to Be Better Coordinated with Key State and Local Information-Sharing Initiatives*, Washington, D.C., GAO-07-455, April 2007.

U.S. House of Representatives, *Conference Report 109-699 on H.R. 5441, Department of Homeland Security Appropriations Act, 2007*, 2006.

Volcker Commission—*see* National Commission on the Public Service.

Wagner, Breanne, "Reluctance to Share Information Hampers Counterterrorism Efforts," *National Defense*, September 2007.

Weick, Karl. E., and Kathleen M. Sutcliffe, *Managing the Unexpected: Assuring High Performance in an Age of Complexity*, San Francisco, Calif.: Jossey-Bass, 2001.

Weick, Karl E., "Leadership When Events Don't Play by the Rules," no date. As of May 14, 2008:
http://www.bus.umich.edu/FacultyResearch/Research/TryingTimes/Rules.htm

———, *Sensemaking in Organizations*, Newbury Park, Calif.: Sage, 1995.

Weisburd, David, and Anthony A. Braga, eds., *Police Innovation: Contrasting Perspectives*, Cambridge, UK: Cambridge University Press, 2006.

Wildhorn, Sorrel, Brian Michael Jenkins, and Marvin Lavin, *Intelligence Constraints of the 1970s and Domestic Terrorism: Volume I, Effects on the Incidence, Investigation, and Prosecution of Terrorist Activity*, Santa Monica, Calif.: RAND Corporation, N-1901-NIJ, December 1982. As of May 14, 2008:
http://www.rand.org/pubs/notes/N1901/

WMD Commission—*see* Commission on the Intelligence Capabilities of the United States Regarding Weapons of Mass Destruction.

Wolf, Paul, "COINTELPRO," Web page, no date. As of May 14, 2008:
http://www.icdc.com/~paulwolf/cointelpro/cointel.htm